LawExpress
LAND LAW

LawExpress
LAND LAW

8th edition

John Duddington
Former Head of the Law School, Worcester College of Technology
Lecturer in Law, University of Worcester

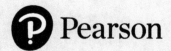
Pearson

Harlow, England • London • New York • Boston • San Francisco • Toronto • Sydney • Dubai • Singapore • Hong Kong
Tokyo • Seoul • Taipei • New Delhi • Cape Town • São Paulo • Mexico City • Madrid • Amsterdam • Munich • Paris • Milan

PEARSON EDUCATION LIMITED
KAO Two
KAO Park
Harlow CM17 9SR
United Kingdom
Tel: +44 (0)1279 623623
Web: www.pearson.com/uk

First published 2007 (print and electronic)
Second edition published 2009 (print and electronic)
Third edition published 2011 (print and electronic)
Fourth edition published 2013 (print and electronic)
Fifth edition published 2015 (print and electronic)
Sixth edition published 2017 (print and electronic)
Seventh edition published 2019 (print and electronic)
Eighth edition published 2021 (print and electronic)

© Pearson Education Limited 2007, 2009, 2011, 2013, 2015, 2017, 2019, 2021 (print and electronic)

ISBN: 978-1-292-29532-9 (print)
        978-1-292-29533-6 (PDF)
        978-1-292-29531-2 (ePub)

British Library Cataloguing-in-Publication Data
A catalogue record for the print edition is available from the British Library

10 9 8 7 6 5 4 3 2 1
25 24 23 22 21

Front cover image: johnnyscriv/E+/Getty Images
Print edition typeset in Janson MT Pro 10/12 by SPi Global

NOTE THAT ANY PAGE CROSS REFERENCES REFER TO THE PRINT EDITION

Contents

Contents

Acknowledgements

Writing Law Express books has now become part of my life and so as ever my thanks go to those who share that life: my wife Anne, for her constant support, loyalty and technical expertise now extending over many years without which my books would never begin to be written; my daughter Mary, for her seemingly faultless proofreading and sense of fun which keeps me going; and my son Christopher for just being himself. In addition I can never forget my father, Walter Duddington, who first encouraged me to become a lawyer, and who would, I am sure, have been a land law enthusiast.

I would also like to thank the staff of Pearson Education for their encouragement, cheerfulness and practical guidance, and the reviewers who sent in such detailed and helpful suggestions for this edition.

Those who know little of land law sometimes think that it inhabits somewhat stagnant waters. Those who read my prefaces to these books will be aware of my view that this is very far from the truth. Since the seventh edition there have been significant developments in virtually every topic covered in this book. Examples are the overruling by the Court of Appeal of the controversial decision in *Baker* v *Craggs*, the significant decision on trusts of the home in *Marr* v *Collie*, proprietary estoppel (*James* v *James* and *Davies* v *Davies*) and the confirmation by the Supreme Court in *Regency Villas Title Ltd* v *Diamond Resorts (Europe) Ltd* of the validity of easements for recreational and sporting use. Meanwhile Parliament has, in the Homes (Fitness for Human Habitation) Act 2018, provided that there is an implied covenant in a lease that a landlord must ensure that the property is fit for human habitation. Moreover, it is gratifying to see so much scholarly writing taking place on land law: I have given references to some of these writings in the hope that students will explore further.

The book is based on materials available to me on the day when it was completed: 5 October 2019.

John Duddington

Former Head of the Law School, Worcester College of Technology
Lecturer in Property Law, University of Worcester

vii

Publisher's acknowledgements

4 The National Archives: Section 205(1)(ix), Law of Property Act (LPA) 1925; **6 The National Archives:** Section 1(1), Law of Property Act 1925; **11 The National Archives:** Section 52(1), Law of Property Act 1925; **11 The National Archives:** Section 1(2) and (3), Law of Property (Miscellaneous Provisions) Act 1989; **14 The National Archives:** Section 2, Law of Property (Miscellaneous Provisions) Act 1989; **14 The National Archives:** Section 2(5), Law of Property (Miscellaneous Provisions) Act 1989; **16 The National Archives:** Section 2(1), Law of Property Act 1925; **18-19 Court of Appeal:** London Borough of Newham v Kibata [2003] EWCA Civ 1785, Mummery LJ in the CA; **19-20 European Court of Human Rights:** FJM v United Kingdom (Admissibility) [2019] H.L.R. 8; **27 House of Commons:** Scheme of the Land Registration Act 2002; **27 The National Archives:** Section 27(1), Land Registration Act 2002; **28 The National Archives:** Section 28, Land Registration Act 2002; **33 The National Archives:** Schedule 3, Paragraph 2, Land Registration Act 2002; **33 Thomson Reuters Corporation:** A Tangled Web of Priority, Conveyancer & Property Lawyer, (2015) p.97; **38 House of Lords:** Abbey National Building Society v Cann [1990] UKHL 3, Lord Oliver; **40 The National Archives:** Section 2(1), Law of Property Act 1925; **58 The National Archives:** Section 34(2), Law of Property Act 1925; **61 Court of Chancery:** Williams v Hensman [1861] EWHC Ch J51; **62 Incorporated Council of Law Reporting (ICLR):** Cowan v Scargill [1985] Ch 270; **62 The National Archives:** Section 6, Trusts of Land and Appointment of Trustees Act 1996; **63 The National Archives:** Section 11(1), Trusts of Land and Appointment of Trustees Act 1996; **64 The National Archives:** Section 15(1), Trusts of Land and Appointment of Trustees Act 1996; **65 Incorporated Council of Law Reporting (ICLR):** Mortgage Corporation v Shaire [2001] Ch 743; **65 LexisNexis:** Bank of Ireland Home Mortgages Ltd v Bell [2001] 2 All ER (Comm) 920 (CA); **74 The National Archives:** Section 53(1)(b), Law of Property Act 1925; **74 The National Archives:** Section 53(2), Law of Property Act 1925; **77 House of Lords:** Stack v Dowden [2007] UKHL 17 (HL); **81 Court of Appeal:** Capehorn v Harris [2015] EWCA Civ 955 (CA); **82 UK Supreme Court:** Jones v Kernott [2011] UKSC 53 (SC); **83 Court of Appeal:** Oxley v Hiscock [2004] EWCA 546, Chadwick LJ; **84 Court of Appeal:** Graham-York v York [2015] EWCA Civ 72, Tomlinson LJ; **92 Royal Courts of Justice:** Thomas v Sorrell [1673] EWHC (KB) Vaughan CJ; **93 Thomson Reuters Corporation:** Cowell v Rosehill Racecourse Co Ltd [1937] 56 CLR 605; **96-97 House of Lords:** Stack v Dowden [2007] UKHL 17 Lord Walker; **98 Chancery Division of the High Court:** James v James [2018] EWHC 43 (Ch).; **101 House of Lords:** Stack v Dowden [2007] UKHL 17; **101 Court of Appeal:** Davies v Davies[2016] EWCA Civ 463 CA; **102 The National Archives:** Section 116, Land Registration Act 2002; **117 Court of Appeal:** Walsh v Lonsdale [1882] 21 Ch D 9 (HC); **121 Court of Appeal:** No.1 West India Quay (Residential) Ltd v East Tower Apartments Ltd [2018] EWCA Civ 250 (CA);

122 Court of Appeal: Kened Ltd and Den Norske Bank plc v Connie Investments Ltd (1997) 04 E.G. 141, Millett LJ; **123 Incorporated Council of Law Reporting (ICLR):** Warren v Keen (1954) QB 15, Denning LJ; **124 Privy Council of the United Kingdom:** Attorney General of Belize v Belize Telecom Ltd [2009] UKPC 10, Lord Hoffman; **124 The National Archives:** Section 5, Landlord and Tenant (Covenants) Act 1995; **126 The National Archives:** Section 141, Law of Property Act 1925; **127 The National Archives:** Section 3, Landlord and Tenant (Covenants) Act 1995; **142 The National Archives:** Section 79(1), Law of Property Act 1925; **143 The National Archives:** Section 56(1), Law of Property Act 1925; **143 Sweet & Maxwell:** Robert Megarry, William Wade (2008) The Law of Real Property. Published by Sweet & Maxwell; **143 The National Archives:** Section 1, Contracts (Rights of Third Parties) Act 1999; **143 The National Archives:** Section 56(1), Contracts (Rights of Third Parties) Act 1999; **146 The National Archives:** Section 79, Law of Property Act 1925; **150 The National Archives:** Section 78(1), Law of Property Act 1925; **152 The National Archives:** Section 84(1), Law of Property Act 1925; **162 LexisNexis:** Copeland v Greenhalf [1952] 1 All ER 809 (HC); **163 House of Lords:** Moncrieff v Jamieson [2007] UKHL 42, Lord Scott; **163 House of Commons:** Law Commission Report, Law Com no 327 Paras 3.199–3.208; **167 The National Archives:** Section 62(1), Law of Property Act 1925; **169 The National Archives:** Section 2, Prescription Act 1832; **170 The National Archives:** Section 3, Prescription Act 1832; **170 The National Archives:** Section 4, Prescription Act 1832; **180 Incorporated Council of Law Reporting (ICLR):** Knightsbridge Estates Trust Ltd v Byrne [1939] Ch 441, Greene MR; **183 House of Lords:** Royal Bank of Scotland plc v Etridge (No 2) [2001] UKHL 44, Lord Nicholls; **187 The National Archives:** Section 36, Administration of Justice Act (AEA) 1970; **188 The National Archives:** Section 101(1) and (4), Law of Property Act 1925; **188 The National Archives:** Section 103, Law of Property Act 1925; **188 Court of Appeal:** Cuckmere Brick Co v Mutual Finance [1971] EWCA Civ 9; **197 Hong Kong Court of Final Appeal:** Powell v McFarlane (1977) 38 P & CR 452, Slade J; **201 LexisNexis:** Pye v Graham [2002] 3 All ER 865 (HL); **207 The National Archives:** Article 1, Human Rights Act 1988.

Introduction

Some general issues

Let us go straight to the point. Students are either land law enthusiasts or they think of land law with fear. This book is intended for both types of student as a guide to how to gain the best possible mark in their exams.

Land law enthusiasts will agree that this is one of the most fascinating of all legal subjects. It is rich in variety, full of interesting issues and, more than in some areas of law, of direct relevance to us all.

Students who fear the subject should remember the following points (enthusiasts will find them useful too):

- There are fewer main cases in land law than in many legal subjects.
- Land law is more statute based than, for example, contract, tort and equity.
- The fact that this is so means that there is more certainty, although it also means that you must be able to recall vital statutory provisions accurately.
- Problem questions are more likely than in some other areas to have a right or wrong answer.

However, there remain two reasons why students do find this subject difficult, and this guide tries to overcome both of them:

(1) The language is off-putting. Terms like 'estates' and 'interests' mysteriously subdivide into 'legal' and 'equitable'. Then land registration rules have terms of their own, such as land charges and overriding interests.

(2) The structure is difficult to understand. How do the basic ideas of estates and interests fit into the land registration rules, and how do the rules themselves work?

These are particular problems in the material covered in the first two chapters: estates and interests in land and registered and unregistered land. Master these and you will have gone a long way to achieving a reasonable pass in your exam, as most questions will involve some knowledge of these areas. Make revision based on these two chapters one of your last jobs before the land law exam.

How does this guide help? It is not a superficial guide which skims the surface of the subject but it aims to help you in the following ways:

- It provides a platform for the study of land law by taking you through the fundamental areas step by step and encourages you not to go on to the next area until you have mastered the one before.
- It links different areas by cross references which clearly point you to other connected areas of the syllabus.
- It highlights key cases, statutes and definitions.
- It gives you tips for the exam based on my forty years' experience as a land law examiner.
- It shows you how each topic develops by a visual map attached to each chapter.
- It gives you suggestions for further reading which will enable you to boost your exam marks.

What this guide *cannot* do is to:

- Do away with the need to learn the material thoroughly and be able to use it in the exam. Only you can do this!
- Act as a substitute for the standard textbooks.

Finally, remember that land law is all around us: when you walk along a footpath you are exercising a right of way; when you pay for a ticket for a football match you are given a contractual licence; when you rent a house you are (probably) entering into a lease. Thinking of the continual relevance of land law makes the subject come alive.

General essay question advice

Answer the actual question and address the issues which it raises. Suppose that you were faced with this question:

> 'The object of the present system of land registration is to ensure that a purchaser will be safe in relying on the register.'
>
> Discuss whether the present system of land registration achieves this aim.

Do not begin by simply describing the system, e.g. by ploughing through overriding interests, etc. Essay questions at this level ask for more than this. *This is the most useful tip for success in answering essay questions.*

Then note that the question refers to the present system, i.e. under the Land Registration Act 2002 – you will get credit for pointing this out – and secondly, *deal with the issue posed in the quotation.* You will get more guidance on this both in this book and on the accompanying website. A useful tip is that land law exams often have an essay question on land registration, so have some points ready!

General problem question advice

In answering any problem question follow these steps. This will get your answer off to a good start:

- Identify the right (Chapter 1 gives a list of proprietary and personal rights – memorise them).
- Check whether any interest in the land is legal or equitable.
- Check whether title to the land is registered or unregistered.

This drill applies throughout the subject, e.g. to questions on leases, licences, easements, profits and mortgages. It will not take you all the way but it will give you a good basis.

Ensure that your answer has a good, logical structure leading to a clear conclusion.

The 'land law box'

When answering problem questions *always* think of *all* the issues in the box (this is the time to think *inside* the box!):

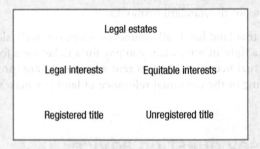

Legal estates

Legal interests   Equitable interests

Registered title   Unregistered title

Also, make sure you are familiar with these two vital statutes:

- Law of Property Act 1925 – still the foundation of land law terminology – abbreviated to LPA 1925 in this book.
- Land Registration Act 2002 – foundation of the system of land registration – abbreviated to LRA 2002 in this book.

About this book

This book is not a potted version of the subject. You will not find within it all the detail you need to pass your exams. It is an aid to learning and not a substitute to reading textbooks, articles (essential if you want a good pass) and, of course, attendance at lectures, tutorials and seminars. It can be used either at the end of the course as a revision aid or during the course to guide you along. Above all it tries to encourage you to *think* about the subject. Thinking students are those who gain the highest marks in exams.

Journals referred to in the 'Key further reading' sections are as follows:

ALJ	*Australian Law Journal*
All ER Review	*All England Law Review*
CLJ	*Cambridge Law Journal*
Conv.	*Conveyancer and Property Lawyer*
LQR	*Law Quarterly Review*
LS	*Legal Studies*
L & T Review	*Land and Tenant Review*
MLR	*Modern Law Review*
SLT	*Scots Law Times*

Throughout your revision, use the questions on the companion website to check your understanding of the subject, and to identify areas where you may want to focus your revision.

Guided tour

How to use features in the book and the companion website.

Understand quickly

Topic maps – Visual guides highlight key subject areas and facilitate easy navigation through the chapter. Download them from the companion website to pin on your wall or add to your revision notes.

Key cases and key statutes – Identify and review the important elements of the essential cases and statutes you will need to know for your exams.

Key further reading – These carefully selected sources will extend your knowledge, deepen your understanding, and help you to earn better marks in coursework and exams.

Glossary – Forgotten the meaning of a word? This quick reference covers key definitions and other useful terms.

Test your knowledge – How well do you know each topic? Test yourself with quizzes tailored specifically to each chapter.

Revise effectively

Revision checklists – Identify essential points you should know for your exams. The chapters will help you revise each point to ensure you are fully prepared. Print the checklists from the companion website to track your progress.

Flashcards – Test and improve recall of important legal terms, key cases and statutes. Available in both electronic and printable formats.

Take exams with confidence

Sample questions with answer guidelines – Practice makes perfect! Consider how you would answer the question at the end of each chapter, then refer to the accompanying answer guidance. Try out additional sample questions online.

Assessment advice – Use this feature to identify how a subject may be examined and how to apply your knowledge effectively.

Impress your examiner – Impress your examiners with these sources of further thinking and debate.

Exam tips – Feeling the pressure? These boxes indicate how you can improve your exam performance when it really counts.

Don't be tempted to – Spot common pitfalls and avoid losing marks.

You be the marker – Evaluate sample exam answers and understand how and why an examiner awards marks.

Table of cases and statutes

Statutes

International Instruments

1

The building blocks
of land law:
estates and interests in land

Revision checklist

Essential points you should know:

- What the terms 'estate', 'freehold' and 'leasehold' mean
- Types of legal interests and equitable interests in land
- When a legal interest binds a third party
- When an equitable interest binds a third party
- When overreaching can apply and its consequences

Topic map

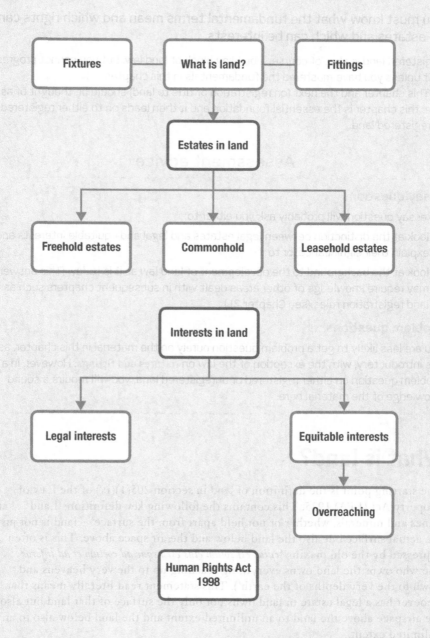

Fixtures — **What is land?** — **Fittings**

Estates in land

Freehold estates — **Commonhold** — **Leasehold estates**

Interests in land

Legal interests — **Equitable interests**

Overreaching

Human Rights Act 1998

A printable version of this topic map is available from **go.pearson.com/uk/lawexpress**

Introduction

You must know what the fundamental terms mean and which rights can be estates and which can be interests.

Registered land is also, of course, a building block of land law, but you cannot progress to it unless you have mastered the fundamentals in this chapter.

This chapter and the next (on registration of title to land) should be thought of as one: this chapter is the essential foundation and it then leads on to either registered or unregistered land.

Assessment advice

Essay questions

An essay question will probably ask you either to:

- look at the distinction between legal estates and legal and equitable interests and explain their significance; or to
- look at the background to the development of land law as it is today. (This answer may require knowledge of other areas dealt with in subsequent chapters such as land registration rules (see Chapter 2).)

Problem questions

You are less likely to get a problem question purely on the material in this chapter, as it is introductory, with the exception of the law on **fixtures and fittings**. However, in a problem question on either registered or unregistered land, you will require a sound knowledge of the material here.

What is land?

The starting point is the definition of **land** in section 205(1)(ix) of the Law of Property Act (LPA) 1925. This contains the following key definition: 'Land . . . and mines and minerals, whether or not held apart from the surface' – land is not just the actual surface but also the land below and the air space above. This is often expressed by the old maxim: '*cuius est solum eius est usque ad coelum et ad inferos*' ('he who owns the land owns everything reaching up to the very heavens and down to the very depths of the earth'). This statement read literally means that whoever has a legal estate in land owns not only the surface of that land but also the airspace above the land to an unlimited extent and the land below also to an unlimited extent.

In *Bocardo SA* v *Star Energy UK Onshore Ltd* (2010) Star Energy had a licence to search for and get petroleum. Its predecessors had drilled three wells diagonally, which entered the substrata below land owned by Bocardo at depths of up to 2,900 feet below ground level but this did not interfere with Bocardo's enjoyment of its land. Nevertheless, Star Energy was held liable for trespass. One issue was the extent to which rights of landowners extended beneath the surface. Lord Hope referred to arguments that the rights should only extend to 1,000 feet below but rejected any definite limit.

The law on rights to the airspace above the ground is different in some respects. Section 76(1) of the Civil Aviation Act 1982 provides that no action shall lie in respect of trespass or nuisance, by reason only of the flight of an aircraft over any property at a height above the ground, which, having regard to wind, weather and all the circumstances of the case is reasonable. In *Bernstein* v *Skyviews and General Ltd* (1978) a claim by a landowner for trespass in respect of flights over his house for aerial photography was rejected. The court held that a landowner only owns such airspace necessary for the reasonable enjoyment of the land.

Impress your examiner

There is a growing literature on subterranean land rights. See Turner (2011).

There is a basic distinction in land law between **corporeal hereditaments** and **incorporeal hereditaments**.

Corporeal hereditaments
The land and what is attached to the land.

Incorporeal hereditaments
Rights over land. These include easements and profits.

Fixtures and fittings

Fixtures are objects which are fixed to the land in such a way as to be part of it. Fittings are not.

Some physical objects are treated as part of the land itself. These are known as fixtures and so when the land is sold anything that is a fixture is sold with it. Other objects are treated as fittings (often referred to as chattels) and are not treated as part of the land. When land is sold, sellers, to avoid disputes, usually provide lists of what are fixtures and fittings.

Botham v *TSB Bank plc* (1996) gives useful guidance on the distinction between fixtures and fittings and a recent case is *Lictor Anstalt* v *Mir Steel UK Ltd* (2014) where a hot strip steel mill used in metalworking processes was a fixture.

The Treasure Act 1996 abolished the old notion of 'treasure trove' and provides that articles defined as treasure vest in the Crown.

Impress your examiner

There is a debate about the notion of property and thus about what are proprietary interests, and you may need to discuss this in an essay question.

Exam tip

In an exam essay question on the nature of property, you should also refer to the change of approach brought about by the Human Rights Act 1998 (see later in this chapter at 'Land law and the Human Rights Act (HRA) 1998').

Estates in land

All land is owned by the Crown. The most that anyone can have is an **estate in land**.

An **estate in land** is the rights which a person has to control and use the land. A **freehold** is a legal estate in land which lasts for an unlimited time and in practice is perpetual. A **leasehold** is a legal estate which lasts for a definite time.

Estates in land must be created by *deed* (see below) except in the case of leases for up to three years (s. 54(2), LPA 1925). Methods of creation of a lease are dealt with in detail in Chapter 6.

Section 1(1), Law of Property Act 1925

The only estates in land which are capable of subsisting or of being created or conveyed at law are:

(a) An estate in **fee simple absolute in possession** (legal freehold estate).

(b) A **term of years absolute** (legal leasehold estate).

Freehold estates

A freehold estate is the nearest to absolute ownership recognised by English law.

Fee simple absolute in possession

The terms together mean:

- **Fee**: can be inherited.
- **Simple**: by anyone.
- **Absolute**: will not end on a certain event, i.e. to x until he marries. This will not qualify.
- **In possession**: not, e.g., to x at 21.

It is possible to have other freehold estates (e.g. for life) but they can only exist behind a **trust** (see later).

All land must have a freehold owner, and if the individual owner cannot be traced the ownership is held by the Crown.

Leasehold estates

Land may also be held under a leasehold estate, and so there may be two estates in the same land.

Term of years absolute

'Term of years' means any period having a fixed and certain duration; 'absolute' appears to have no meaning beyond the fact that a term of years may be absolute even if it contains a clause enabling either party to determine it by notice.

Impress your examiner

You may get an essay question on the historical development of land law, so consider:

- Why was the LPA 1925 passed?
- Does it need further reform?

This will be linked with the system of land registration – in particular, this has been updated by the Land Registration Act (LRA) 2002 (see Chapter 2). For a good mark, look at Simpson (1986).

Commonhold

The concept of **commonhold** was introduced by the Commonhold and Leasehold Reform Act 2002. You are less likely to get a whole question on this, but an answer to an essay question on the general principles of land law will gain extra marks if you mention commonhold. The basic idea is that where land is divided into separate units (e.g. flats), but there are also common parts (e.g. lifts, stairways), then there can be another means of holding land as distinct from the traditional freehold and leasehold. Under this scheme, individuals will own a unit (e.g. their flat) but the common parts will be owned and managed by a commonhold association. The distinctive feature is that there is no external party such as a landlord, where there is a lease. It is believed that there are fewer than 50 blocks of flats in England and Wales in commonhold. The Law Commission (2018) is engaged on a project to see if commonhold can be made a more attractive alternative to leasehold. It intends to publish its final report in February 2020.

Impress your examiner

See Land Practice Registry Guide 60. You will incidentally find Land Practice Registry Guides an invaluable resource in your studies of land law for a discussion and analysis of commonhold.

Interests in land

An interest in land is a right which a person has over another's land. Remember that an estate in land is a right which a person has over his or her own land.

There are two types of **interests in land**:

(1) Legal interests
(2) Equitable interests.

Those interests which are legal are set out below and all other interests must be equitable. Do not think about equitable interests until you have mastered legal interests.

Legal and equitable interests in land have one common feature: they are **proprietary rights** in land. These must be distinguished from **personal rights**.

Proprietary rights are those capable of binding third parties, i.e. legal estates and legal and equitable interests in land (see Example 1.1). Personal rights are not capable of binding third parties, e.g. licences.

Example 1.1

Z has an easement over X's land. This is an example of a proprietary right and so is capable of binding Y when X sells his land to Y.

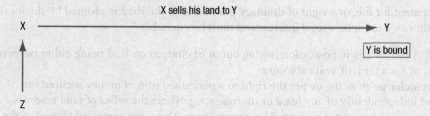

Z has permission from X to sit in X's garden and paint the view of the hills. This is only a licence and so it is a personal right and cannot be binding on Y.

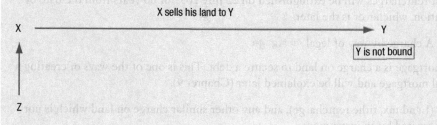

Legal interests in land

These are defined in section 1(2) of the LPA 1925. Only these can be legal. All interests not in this list must be equitable. **Legal interests** bind all the world, i.e. everyone who buys the land, subject to the land registration rules.

Exam tip

For an essay question you should know all the legal interests but only the interests in (a) and (c) below (easements, profits and mortgages) are likely to appear in problem questions.

The list of interests that can be legal is:

(a) An **easement**, right or privilege in or over land for an interest equivalent to an estate in fee simple absolute in possession or a term of years absolute.

This includes both easements and **profits** *à prendre*. An **easement** gives the right to use the land of another in some way, or to prevent it from being used for certain purposes, e.g. rights of way and rights of water and light. **Profits** give the right to take something from the land of another, e.g. peat, fish, wood or grazing rights.

You need to be absolutely clear about the distinction between these. Easements and profits are dealt with in Chapter 8.

However, to be legal, the right must be held either for an indefinite time (equivalent to a fee simple) or for a definite time (equivalent to a term of years). Therefore, an easement for life, or a right of drainage granted until the road is adopted by the local authority, cannot be a legal interest and must be equitable.

(b) A rentcharge in possession issuing out of or charged on land being either perpetual or for a term of years absolute.

A rentcharge gives the owner the right to a periodical sum of money secured on land independently of any lease or mortgage, e.g. where the seller of land reserves an annual payment for it secured by a rentcharge. These are commonly found in the Manchester and Bristol areas.

No new rentcharges can be created after 22 July 1977 (with certain exceptions) and most rentcharges will be extinguished on 22 July 2037 or 60 years from the date of creation, whichever is the later.

(c) A charge by way of legal mortgage.

A mortgage is a charge on land to secure a debt. This is one of the ways of creating a legal mortgage and will be explained later (Chapter 9).

(d) (Land tax, tithe rentcharge), and any other similar charge on land which is not created by an instrument.

The common feature of any charges coming within this provision is that they are periodical payments with which land was burdened by law. The (specific charges) that fell within this provision have been abolished.

(e) Rights of entry exercisable over or in respect of a legal term of years absolute, or annexed, for any purpose, to a legal rentcharge.

A right of re-entry in a lease – e.g., if the tenant fails to pay the rent – is made an interest in land in itself. It can be attached to a legal rentcharge to secure payment of the rent.

Exam tip

The most common legal interests for exam purposes are in categories (a) and (c) above.

Assuming that the interest is within this list, then in order to be legal it must have been created by deed.

Section 52(1), Law of Property Act 1925

Requires the use of a deed to create or convey a legal estate or interest in land.

A deed is a document which, if made before 31 July 1990, had to be sealed but this is no longer necessary.

Section 1(2) and (3), Law of Property (Miscellaneous Provisions) Act 1989

An instrument shall not be a deed unless:

- it makes clear that it is intended to be a deed;
- it is signed by the person executing it and by a witness present at the same time who also signs it;
- it is delivered by the person executing it or by someone on his behalf.

Example 1.2(a)

X agrees with Y by a deed that Y can have a right of way across X's land for the rest of Y's life.

Step one: Identify the right – an easement.

Step two: Is it legal or equitable? As it is for life, it can only be equitable, even if it is in a deed.

Example 1.2(b)

X agrees with Y by a deed that Y can have a right of way across X's land.

Step one: Identify the right – an easement.

Step two: Is it legal or equitable? As it does not say that the easement is only for Y's life, we can assume that it is for ever. Therefore it is a legal easement.

Step three: Is it in a deed? Yes, so it is legal.

Note: Sometimes the interest is not actually granted by deed but is implied into it or presumed. See Chapter 8 for examples in connection with easements.

Equitable interests in land

All other interests in land are equitable.

The term **equitable interests** means that the right was originally only recognised by the Court of Chancery, which dealt with equitable rights, and not by the Courts of Common Law.

You do not need to know **equity** in detail in order to pass exams in land law, but you should keep the following fundamental characteristic of equity in mind.

Equity often applied where the application of the strict rules of the common law would not have produced a just result. The effect was that equity often did not insist on the observance of formalities, such as the need for a right to be granted in a deed (above). You can find out more about equity in the companion Law Express book to this one: *Equity and Trusts*.

Don't be tempted to . . .

Make sure that you revise the rules for deciding whether an interest is equitable or not. In land law exams you should ask two questions to decide if the right is equitable:

- Is it in the above list of legal interests? If not, then it must be equitable.
- If it is in the above list, then was it created by deed? If not, then it can only be equitable.

Chapter 2 also deals with another way in which a right can become equitable rather than legal: if it is not registered as required by the LRA 2002. Keep this point at the back of your mind for now, but do not worry about registered land yet.

Interests under trusts

A **trust** arises when property is held by one person (the trustee) on trust for another (the beneficiary).

X (trustee) ————————————————————▶ Y (beneficiary)

X is the legal owner but Y has the equitable interest.

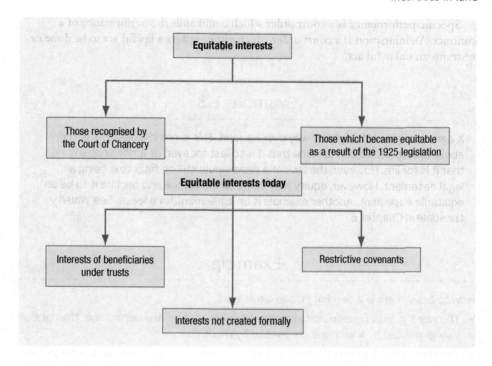

Therefore, the legal ownership and the benefit are split, and the common law – apparently because it could not cope with the idea of splitting these two – refused to recognise trusts and allowed the **trustee** to ignore the rights of the **beneficiaries**. Equity, however, enforced trusts because this was a matter of conscience, i.e. the trustee had never been intended to have complete control of the property. You will find later that a trustee can also be a beneficiary, if this was intended.

A common example of a trust is where a person (X) contributes to the purchase of land but the legal title is held in the name of Y. Y will hold the land on trust for X in the absence of a contrary intention. See Chapters 2, 3 and 4. Keep this example of a trust in mind: it is frequently met in land law.

Interests not created formally

If a contract has been made to create an interest in land then equity may, at its discretion, enforce it by a decree of **specific performance** or restrain its breach by an **injunction**. This is in accordance with the equitable maxim that 'equity looks on that as done which ought to be done'. This means that when a deed is required to create an estate or interest in land and there is no deed, equity may still regard the interest subsisting in land as an equitable interest.

Specific performance is a court order which commands the performance of a contract. An injunction is a court order which either orders a lawful act to be done or restrains an unlawful act.

Example 1.3

- -

X agrees to grant Y a right of way over his land. This is not in a deed. As in the above examples, we can assume that it is to last for ever, as it does not say that it is for life. However, the lack of a deed would still be fatal to it being a legal easement. However, equity may come to the rescue and declare it to be an equitable easement. Another example is an agreement for a lease. See *Walsh* v *Lonsdale* in Chapter 6.

Exam tip

- -

How to tell if there is a deed or just an agreement:

- The word 'grants' usually indicates a deed, as this is the idea behind one: the right of way is granted by X to Y and not agreed by them.

- The term 'agrees to grant' indicates just an agreement as it points to the future, and this fits with the idea behind equity: it enforces a contract to grant an interest in the future.

- -

Section 2, Law of Property (Miscellaneous Provisions) Act 1989

Section 2(1) provides that contracts for the sale or other disposition of an interest in land made on or after 27 September 1989 must:

- be in writing;
- contain all the terms agreed by the parties; and
- be signed by all the parties.

Note also section 2(5) '. . . nothing in this section affects the creation or operation of resulting, implied or constructive trusts'. This is considered in Chapter 5.

Therefore, equity will, for example, enforce a contract for an equitable easement provided that it satisfies these requirements. Contracts made before that date do not require writing. Another example of an equitable interest in this connection is an estate contract, which is a contract to convey a legal estate.

If an agreement does not satisfy the requirements of section 2(1) of the Law of Property (Miscellaneous) Provisions Act, then it may still be enforceable under the principles of constructive trusts, see section 2(5) above and Chapter 5.

In *Keay* v *Morris Homes (West Midlands) Ltd* [2012] it was held that any agreement to vary the sale agreement had to be contained in a document satisfying section 2 because by agreeing to vary the contract, the parties were in effect entering into a new contract.

Electronic conveyancing

Section 91 of the LRA 2002 provides that, in order to pave the way for the introduction of electronic conveyancing, electronic documents will be capable of satisfying the formality requirements for deeds and contracts set out above.

E-conveyancing was intended as a complete electronic system of conveyancing from the initial offer to purchase to registration of title but a statutory scheme has not been introduced. The Law Commission Report (2018) Updating Land Registration (LC 380) proposed the introduction of e-conveyancing with the present system continuing for now to operate alongside it.

Restrictive covenants

Where a person covenants in a deed not to use his land in a certain way or to do something on his land – e.g. to keep fences in repair or not to build on the land. See Chapter 7.

These have only ever been enforced in equity.

Why do you need to know the distinction between legal and equitable interests?

Because of the different effect they have on a purchaser of the land. When you read Chapter 2, you will see the significance of the distinction between legal and equitable interests.

Note that if a person is not the purchaser, but has acquired the land by gift or by inheritance, then that person takes the land with all equitable rights.

Exam tip

Check in a question whether a person, for instance, inherited the land. If so, he or she will not be a purchaser.

Overreaching

The process by which equitable rights that exist under a trust of land are removed from the land and transferred to the money (called capital money) that has been paid to purchase the land. The effect is to give the purchaser automatic priority over equitable interests under a trust.

Section 2(1), Law of Property Act 1925

'A conveyance to a purchaser of a legal estate in land shall overreach any equitable interest or power affecting the estate, whether he has notice thereof . . .' There are various instances where overreaching can take place, but the relevant one here is section 2(1)(ii): where the provisions of section 27 of the LPA 1925 regarding the payment of capital money are complied with, i.e. the capital money is paid to at least two trustees or a trust corporation.

Note carefully this vital restriction on **overreaching**: it can only take place if the transaction is made by at least two trustees or a trust corporation.

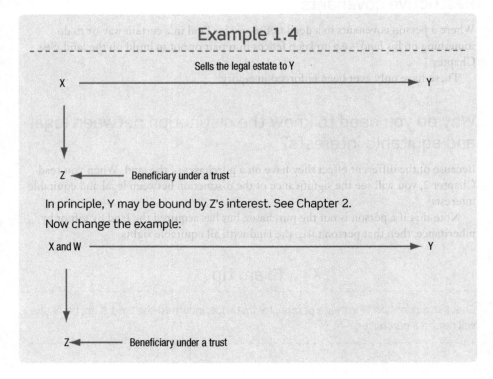

Example 1.4

Sells the legal estate to Y

X ────────────────────────────────► Y

Z ◄──────── Beneficiary under a trust

In principle, Y may be bound by Z's interest. See Chapter 2.

Now change the example:

X and W ────────────────────────────► Y

Z ◄──────── Beneficiary under a trust

Here Y will not be bound by Z's interest as the transaction was entered into by two trustees (X and W) and so Z's interest in the property is overreached and is transferred to the proceeds of sale. The effect is that Y need not concern himself about Z's interest but Z may claim against X and W for any share of the proceeds of sale which she feels belongs to her.

Exam tip

If you get a problem question on the rights of beneficiaries under a trust of land (see Chapter 2) check first how many persons are transferring the legal estate. If it is one, there cannot be overreaching but see *Shami* v *Shami* discussed later in this chapter. If there are more than one, overreaching will take place.

City of London Building Society v *Flegg* [1987] 3 All ER 435 (HL)

Facts

Mr and Mrs MB were the registered proprietors of a house, but over half the purchase price had been raised by Mr and Mrs F, the parents of Mrs MB, who were also to live at the house. Accordingly, the house was held on trust for all four of them. Mr and Mrs MB then, without the knowledge of Mrs MB's parents, raised two further charges over the property and then defaulted on the repayments. The lender sought possession and it was held that the interests of the parents had been overreached by the charges and that their rights now only existed in the proceeds of sale.

Legal principle

The interests of beneficiaries in a trust of land are overreached if the transaction is, in this case, entered into by two or more trustees.

Analysis

This decision fits with the policy of the 1925 legislation in keeping trusts of land 'behind the curtain' so that investigation of the legal title is confined to the legal estate. However, the practical result, that the ability of beneficiaries to stay in the home depends on whether more than one trustee conveys the land, is not easy to uphold in terms of justice.

Note that under section 205(1)(xxi) of the LPA 1925, a purchaser includes a chargee by way of legal mortgage, i.e. in practice, a lender under a mortgage.

Recent case law is extending the cases where overreaching can take place and some clarification of this area of the law is needed. Note:

State Bank of India v *Sood* (1997): overreaching applies not only where capital money is actually paid, but also where the mortgage was created as security for both existing and future liabilities. Thus, at the time, no capital money (i.e. mortgage finance here) changed hands.

Shami v *Shami* (2012): held **obiter** that even where the sale is by one owner beneficial interests can be overreached where no capital money arises on the sale. The implications of this are considered in Chapter 2.

Mortgage Express v *Lambert* (2016): not only beneficial interests under a trust can be overreached, but also a right to set aside the sale on the grounds that it was an unconscionable bargain, known as a '**mere equity**'.

Baker v *Craggs* (2016): the High Court had held that overreaching was triggered by the grant of an easement by two trustees to X rather than, as in all other cases, the grant of a freehold or leasehold. This was overruled by the Court of Appeal which held that section 2(1) of the LPA 1925 applied only upon a conveyance to a purchaser of a legal estate in land, and an easement was not a 'legal estate in land'. For more on this case see Chapter 2.

Impress your examiner

View overreaching in its social context by pointing out that as a result of the rising cost of home ownership the *Flegg* situation may become more common. Read too Owen (2015). A new model for overreaching – some historical inspiration. 79 *Conv.* 226 who proposes that, in the context of registered land, the current overreaching rules would only apply if the particular beneficial interest had not been registered. Thus the onus would be on registration.

Land law and the Human Rights Act (HRA) 1998

This can be relevant to a land law exam in two ways:

(1) As a separate essay question.

(2) To mention when you are looking at a specific area, e.g. overreaching (see above), discharge of a restrictive covenant under section 84 of the LPA 1925 (see Chapter 7) and adverse possession (see Chapter 10). You can boost your marks here by mentioning this Act.

Think of this quote from Mummery LJ in the CA in *Newham LBC* v *Kibata* (2003), who considered that the HRA has 'brought about a new species of property right in the home'. At a wider level the debate is about the place, not only of land law, but of law itself, in society.

Article 8 of the ECHR (respect for family and private life) has been relied on by tenants against landlords seeking possession because Art. 8 requires the courts to engage in a proportionality exercise (as provided for by Art. 8(2)) in addition to applying any statutory protections available to the tenant. There was a good deal of case law on this area with differing judicial approaches but the leading authority in possession cases is now this case.

***

Manchester City Council v Pinnock [2011] UKSC 6

Facts
Manchester City Council sought to evict Pinnock from a property owned by them because of a number of incidents of serious anti-social behaviour caused by members of his family.

Legal principle
A person at risk of being dispossessed of her home by a public authority should have the right to question the proportionality of this interference with her Art. 8 ECHR right to respect for that home before an independent tribunal. However, on the facts here such an argument had no real prospect of success.

Analysis
The effect is to give domestic courts jurisdiction under the ECHR where a person at risk of being dispossessed of their home by a local authority questions the proportionality of that decision under Art. 8. As such it is a landmark case and has been followed subsequently.

***

Pinnock concerned a public sector tenant and the SC left open whether Art. 8 had horizontal effect in these cases, i.e. between a private landlord and a tenant, but in *McDonald* v *McDonald* (2016) the Supreme Court held that it did not. The general presumption against horizontal effect was bolstered by the fact that the contractual rights of tenants had been considered by Parliament and subject to statutory regulation. There was no 'clear and constant' ECtHR case law establishing an Art. 8 defence in purely private proceedings.

In *FJM* v *United Kingdom (Admissibility)* (2019) the ECtHR rejected an appeal from this decision and held that: 'What sets claims for possession by private sector owners against residential occupiers apart is that the two private individuals or entities have entered voluntarily into a contractual relationship in respect of which the legislature has prescribed how their respective Convention rights are to be respected. If the domestic courts could override the balance struck by the legislation in such a case, the Convention would be directly enforceable between private citizens so as to alter the contractual rights and obligations that they had freely entered into.'

See Loveland (2017) who not only looks at the recent litigation but provides a clear account of this whole area and Maxwell (2019) on the ECtHR decision.

The Law Commission (2011) Report 327, Making land work: easements, covenants and profits *à prendre*, mentions at paragraph 1.32 that care was taken not to disturb existing property rights, partly at least because of Article 1 of the First Protocol of the ECHR which provides that no one shall be deprived of his or her possessions except in the public interest and subject to the conditions provided for by law.

Ownership, possession and occupation

Impress your examiner

English common law has historically emphasised possession of land rather than ownership. Indeed, as explained above, no one can actually own land. Emphasis on possession is still true today; for example, a person will not have a leasehold estate unless he or she is granted exclusive possession of the leasehold property (see Chapter 6). The common law's emphasis on possession as the basis of title is now giving way to a state-regulated system based on land registration.

Distinguish possession from occupation – an occupier may or may not have both possession and a legal estate in the land. A personal occupier who does not have exclusive possession will have just a licence (see Chapter 6); however, an occupier with a proprietary (not just personal) interest in the land may have a right which binds those who acquire the land – see overriding interests in Chapter 2.

Putting it all together

Sample question

Could you answer this question? Below is a typical essay question which could arise on this topic. Additionally, a sample problem question and guidance on tackling it can be found on the companion website.

Essay question

- -

Distinguish between legal and equitable interests in land. What is the importance of the distinction?

- -

Answer guidelines

Approaching the question

This question should be relatively straightforward as it just requires you to recognise legal and equitable interests in land and distinguish between them.

Important points to include

- Begin by giving a clear explanation of what these terms mean, avoiding too much elaboration – never neglect basic points!
- Then go through the main examples of each, aiming above all here for accuracy because you will need to apply these rules in more complex situations later and you must get these 'building blocks' right.
- Then explain the importance of the distinction, i.e. the effect on third-party rights. Again, clear and accurate explanations please!

Impress your examiner

- -

At this stage an answer will stand out if it just shows a clear grasp of the issues and, if possible, an exploration of the case law on the meaning of 'notice' in connection with equitable interests in unregistered land (see Chapter 2).

Key case summary

Key case	How to use	Related topics
City of London Building Society v *Flegg*	To show how the principle of overreaching operates.	Overriding interests.
Manchester City Council v *Pinnock*	Application of Article 8 of the ECHR to possession proceedings.	The effect of the Human Rights Act 1998 on land law.

Key further reading

Key articles/reports	How to use	Related topics
Loveland, I. (2017) Twenty years later: assessing the significance of the Human Rights Act in possession proceedings. 3. *Conv.* 174.	This is an absolutely essential survey of the ways in which the courts have approached actions for possession where Art. 8 of the ECHR may be engaged.	Land Law and Human Rights.
Maxwell, S. (2019) The end of the road for proportionality review when hearing claims for possession by private sector landlords? 5 *JPL* 435.	This looks at the litigation in *McDonald* v *McDonald* including the decision in the ECtHR.	Land Law and Human Rights.
Simpson, A. (1986) *A History of the Land Law, 2nd edn.* Oxford: Oxford University Press, especially pp. 242–92, Chapters X and XI.	Although land law syllabuses often have less historical content today this area remains rooted in history and reading this book will give you very valuable insights and so boost your marks in the exam.	History and context of land law.
Turner, A. (2011) Below the law? Issues in subterranean law and practice. 6 *Conv.* 465.	This looks at problems where rights below the land are claimed – an increasingly important area.	Rights under the land.

go.pearson.com/uk/lawexpress

Go online to access more revision support including quizzes to test your knowledge, sample questions with answer guidelines, printable versions of the topic maps, and more!

2

Registered and unregistered title to land

Revision checklist

Essential points you should know:

- What is meant by registration of titles to land and how this differs from unregistered title to land
- Which dispositions must be completed by registration
- What is meant by the term 'interests which can override'
- What is meant by the term 'protected registered interests' and how such interests can be protected
- Which rights must be registered as land charges to bind a purchaser
- Whether purchasers are bound by legal interests and equitable interests which are not registrable as land charges

Topic map

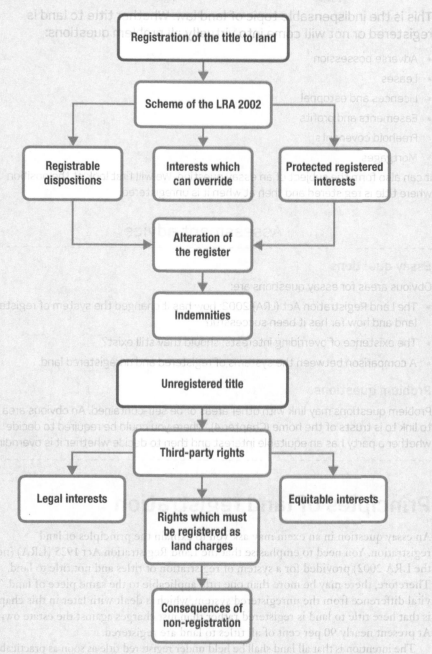

A printable version of this topic map is available from **go.pearson.com/uk/lawexpress**

Introduction

This is the indispensable topic of land law. Whether title to land is registered or not will come into virtually all problem questions:

- Adverse possession
- Leases
- Licences and estoppel
- Easements and profits
- Freehold covenants
- Mortgages.

It can also form the subject of an essay question. We will first look at the position where title is registered and then at when it is unregistered.

Assessment advice

Essay questions

Obvious areas for essay questions are:

- The Land Registration Act (LRA) 2002: how has it changed the system of registered land and how far has it been successful?
- The existence of overriding interests: should they still exist?
- A comparison between the systems of registered and unregistered land.

Problem questions

Problem questions may link with other areas or be self-contained. An obvious area to link to is trusts of the home (Chapter 4), where you could be required to decide whether a party has an equitable interest and then to decide whether it is overriding.

Principles of land registration

An essay question in an exam may ask you to explain the principles of land registration. You need to emphasise that the Land Registration Act 1925 (LRA) (now the LRA 2002) provided for a system of registration of titles and not title to land. Therefore, there may be more than one title applicable to the same piece of land. The vital difference from the unregistered system, which is dealt with later in this chapter, is that here title to land is registered rather than just charges against the estate owner. At present nearly 90 per cent of all titles to land are registered.

The intention is that all land shall be held under registered title as soon as practicable.

The other main aim of the LRA 2002 is to make arrangements to the legislation to enable dispositions of registered land to be dealt with electronically. See Chapter 1.

The land registration scheme rests on three principles:

(1) **Mirror principle** – all facts relevant to the title are to be found on the register.

(2) **Curtain principle** – purchasers need not look beyond the register and are not concerned with trusts.

(3) **Insurance principle** – any flaw in the register leads to the payment of compensation to a person affected.

Scheme of the Land Registration Act 2002

The LRA 2002 takes the different types of estates and interests in land (see Chapter 1) and classifies them for the purposes of land registration in the following ways:

- Dispositions which must be completed by registration.
- Unregistered dispositions which override registered dispositions. These correspond to the old category of overriding interests (see later) and the effect is that a buyer of the land can be bound by an interest that is not on the register. This is a highly significant area and often forms the subject of examination questions. We shall continue to refer to these as overriding interests.
- Interests that must be protected by an entry against the title which they bind. These were formerly known as *minor interests*.

These categories will be explored in detail later, but it is absolutely essential that you know them and can apply them in an exam.

Exam tip

A thorough knowledge of the three ways in which the LRA 2002 classifies estates and interests in land will gain you marks in virtually all problem questions in the exam, not just questions specifically on land registration.

Registrable dispositions

> ### Section 27(1), Land Registration Act 2002
>
> If a disposition is required to be completed by registration, then it does not operate at all until it is registered in accordance with the requirements.

A registrable disposition is one that must be completed by registration.

The dispositions that must be completed by registration are set out in section 27 of the LRA:

- **Transfer of the registered freehold estate.** This includes transfers by any of the following methods:
  (a) for valuable or other consideration;
  (b) by way of gift;
  (c) in pursuance of a court order;
  (d) transfer by personal representatives on death.
- **The grant of a legal lease with more than seven years to run.** In addition, certain leases for less than seven years are registrable, e.g. those which take effect more than three months after the date of the grant.
- **Certain other leases and rights arising under leases**, e.g. registration of the grant of a right to buy a lease under the Housing Act 1985.
- **The express grant or reservation of legal easements, legal profits, legal rentcharges.**
- **A first legal mortgage created out of the estate.** This will apply whenever existing legal mortgages are discharged and a new mortgage is created. This rule has proved to be one of the main means of transferring land from the unregistered system to the registered system.

The above are the 'triggers' to registration of title. They cover almost all the possibilities but not quite: when an unregistered freehold or leasehold estate with less than seven years to run is transferred to a new trustee by deed or vesting order.

Don't be tempted to ...

Be sure that you understand the *relationship* between section 28 and section 29 of the LRA 2002.

Section 28, Land Registration Act 2002

This sets out the basic rule: the priority of an interest affecting a registered estate or charge is not affected by a disposition of the estate or charge. The effect is that priority of interests in registered land depends on their date of creation.

Before you try to make sense of this, turn to:

Section 29, Land Registration Act 2002

This section provides (not the exact words) that the effect of a registered disposition made for *valuable consideration* (my italics) is that it takes priority over any rights affecting the estate prior to the disposition which are not protected by registration or are overriding. Thus, an interest which is neither overriding nor protected by an entry on the register will not be binding on the purchaser.

The relationship between sections 28 and 29 can be seen in this example.

Example 2.1

John, the registered proprietor of Blackacre, has made a contract to sell it to Mary.

(a) John dies and Anne inherits Blackacre. Mary's contract binds Anne as Mary's right was created first. This is section 28.

(b) John sells Blackacre to Anne. As the disposition was for valuable consideration (the word 'sells' indicates this), section 29 applies and, if Mary's contract was not protected by registration, it will not bind Anne.

The relationship between section 28 and section 29 was considered in *Halifax plc v Curry Popeck* (2008), where the issue was the priority of two mortgages to different lenders over a property. The property had been transferred fraudulently and therefore no question of valuable consideration arose, so section 28 applied. Thus the mortgage created first had priority. Although the first lender had not acquired an immediate charge over the property as there was no contract to satisfy section 2 of the Law of Property (Miscellaneous Provisions) Act 1989, the first lender did have a right by proprietary estoppel.

Section 28 can apply in a problem involving adverse possession (see Chapter 10) as well as, of course, in other areas, so check whether a person has acquired the land by gift (which includes inheritance). If it was acquired by sale, section 29 applies.

The net effect of all this is that the basic rule in section 28 is an exception and usually section 29 applies as the land will have been sold and not given away.

Note that the effect of sections 27 and 29 of the 2002 Act is that, although a registrable disposition takes place when it is executed, neither a conveyance nor a charge takes effect at law until registration, and so a purchaser and a mortgagee acquire only equitable interests on completion until registration.

There are a few dispositions concerning freehold land or leases for at least seven years which will not be caught by the above rules and which will not need to be registered. One example is an assignment of a mortgage.

Voluntary registration is also possible, e.g. a freehold estate may be registered even though it is not being transferred.

Exam tip

When revising, remember sections 27, 28 and 29 – these are all vital sections of the LRA 2002.

Overriding interests

Exam tip

This is probably the most common topic on registered land for both essay questions and problem questions.

An overriding interest is an unregistered disposition which overrides a registered disposition.

The LRA 2002 distinguishes between:

- interests which override on first registration of the land; and
- interests which override on subsequent registration of the land.

Why?

This is because the effect of a first and a subsequent registration is different:

Example 2.2(a)

John sells 112 High Street, which has unregistered title, to Mary. Following the sale, Mary registers the title. John's son Christopher, who contributed to the purchase price when John bought the house, still lives there. Christopher may have an equitable interest in the property. It is not at this time an overriding interest as title to 112 High Street has not been registered. The time for deciding if Christopher's interest is binding on Mary is when Mary acquired the title to it and the principles of unregistered land are relevant – see the diagram. However, when Mary's title is registered later, Christopher's interest may then count as an overriding interest.

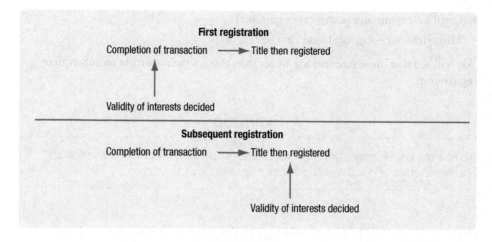

Example 2.2(b)

Now the title is registered. The crucial time in this example is when Mary's title is registered. Christopher's interest now counts as an overriding interest throughout the transaction.

Impress your examiner

See Law Commission (2001), Paper 271, especially paragraph 8.3.

Exam tip

If a problem question says that the title to land *is* registered and then asks you about, for example, the effect on third-party rights of a sale, that sale will result in a subsequent registration.

Interests which override on first registration

- Legal leases not exceeding seven years
- Interests of persons in actual occupation

- Legal easements and profits (not equitable)
- Miscellaneous – e.g. local land charges.

You will see that these interests are wider than those which override on subsequent registration.

Exam tip

When there is a first registration, the interests of persons in actual occupation are binding whether or not the occupier has made enquiries of them.

Interests which override on subsequent registration

This will be the most important category in exams and will be dealt with in much more detail.

Leases

- Legal leases with more than seven years to run are registrable dispositions.
- Legal leases not exceeding seven years are overriding interests (Sch. 3, Para. 1, LRA 2002).
- Equitable leases should be protected by registration (estate contracts); but if they are not, and if the leaseholder is in actual occupation, then they may have an overriding interest under Schedule 3, Paragraph 2, LRA 2002, below.

Note: section 118(1) of the LRA 2002 gives the Lord Chancellor the power to reduce the period for which registration of a legal lease is required. It is likely to be reduced to three years.

Overriding interests of occupiers
Exam tip

Cases on this area are often a contest between a person with a beneficial interest in property and a lender who wishes to enforce a charge under a mortgage on that property. Who should have priority? Keep this in mind.

Schedule 3, Paragraph 2, Land Registration Act 2002

An interest belonging at the time of the disposition to a person in actual occupation except for:

(i) an interest of a person of whom enquiry was made before the disposition and who failed to disclose the right when he could have been reasonably expected to do so;

(ii) an interest which belongs to a person whose occupation would not have been obvious on a reasonable inspection of the land at the time of the disposition and of which the person to whom the disposition was made does not have actual knowledge.

In *Begum* v *Issa* (2014) it was held that an enquiry about a person's interest made at a party was not enough to prevent an overriding interest arising. Thus as Dixon (A Tangled Web of Priority, (2015) 2 *Conv.* 97) puts it: 'the adequacy of the alleged enquiry must be judged according to the circumstances in which it is made and the relationship of the parties to the discussion'. See *Trevallion* v *Watmore* (2016), a decision of the First Tier Tribunal, for an interesting example of what may constitute a 'reasonable inspection'.

Exam tip

- -

This area will come up somewhere in your exam either as:

- a direct question on land registration; or, for example:
- in a question on adverse possession; or
- in a question on leases, easements or profits.

- -

Impress your examiner

- -

The law changed from the LRA 1925 when the corresponding provision (s. 70(1)(g), LRA 1925) did not provide that an overriding interest could be lost in Schedule 3, Paragraph 2 case (ii) above. The new provision has in effect introduced the idea of notice found in unregistered land to registered land. This is controversial. Read the articles suggested in the 'Key further reading' section at the end of this chapter.

You should approach a problem question based on the cases below in this way.

When does a right qualify as for overriding status?

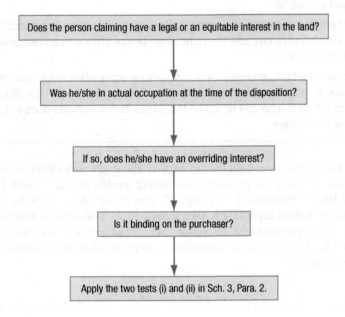

Does the person claiming have a legal or an equitable interest in the land?

Was he/she in actual occupation at the time of the disposition?

If so, does he/she have an overriding interest?

Is it binding on the purchaser?

Apply the two tests (i) and (ii) in Sch. 3, Para. 2.

National Provincial Bank v *Ainsworth* (1965): held that this applies where there is a proprietary interest in land, whether it is legal or equitable. Although this case was decided under the LRA 1925, the principle is still valid and was given statutory force by section 29(1) of the LRA 2002 (see earlier) which refers to any interest '*affecting the estate*', i.e. a proprietary interest. In many cases, the interest has arisen under a resulting or constructive trust where the party claiming has, for example, contributed to the cost of acquisition of the property but it is not owned by them. However, in some recent cases, e.g. *Thompson* v *Foy* (2009) and *Link Lending Ltd* v *Hussein* (2010) (later in this chapter) the interest arose through a claimed right to set a sale aside through undue influence.

Williams & Glyn's Bank v Boland [1980] 2 All ER 408 (HL)

Facts
The wife had contributed to the purchase price of property and so had acquired a beneficial interest in it. The husband mortgaged it to the bank which sought possession when he did not keep up the repayments.

Legal principle
As the wife was in occupation under an equitable interest (i.e. a proprietary interest), she had an overriding interest which bound the bank.

Analysis
This was a ground-breaking decision in protecting rights of occupation especially of partners who had contributed in some way to the purchase price of the family home but who were not registered as owners. The HL emphasised the fact of occupation as being the vital factor rather than whether the purchaser (often in this context the mortgagee) had notice of the equitable interest under which the occupier was in occupation. To evaluate the significance of this case, compare it with *Caunce* v *Caunce* (1969).

The situation in this case and other similar ones can be seen in this way and you may find it useful to make a similar diagram when you get a problem question on this area:

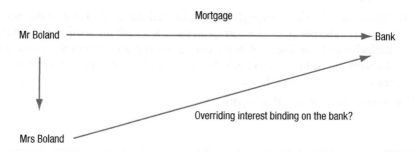

Exam tip

A problem question may ask you to discuss in more detail whether a person in Mrs Boland's position does have an equitable interest. Check Chapter 4 and make sure that you are clear on the principles in *Stack* v *Dowden* and *Jones* v *Kernott*.

There are three issues to focus on:

(a) What is meant by occupation? Although cases decided under the LRA 1925 are worth mentioning, it is especially important to be aware of recent case law where this term has been considered in the context of the Land Registration Act 2002.

In *Williams & Glyn's Bank* v *Boland* (1980) Lord Wilberforce explained that the word 'actual' meant that physical presence was required. Can occupation be lost by temporary absence? Consider *Chhokar* v *Chhokar* (1984). Cases under the 2002 Act have included:

(i) *Link Lending Ltd* v *Hussein* (2010) where the claimant was in actual occupation, even though she was involuntarily detained under the Mental Health Act, as she intended to return to the property when it was possible. Also, her possessions were still there.

(ii) *Thomas* v *Clydesdale Bank plc* (2010) where there was occupation even though the house was being renovated: the court held that the degree of occupation must take into account that the house was not being used as a residence on the date of the disposition but the claimant was present at the property almost daily during renovation.

(iii) *Chaudhary* v *Yavuz* (2013) where the claim was based on an equitable easement allowing use of a staircase giving access to the upper floors of a flat via a balcony. However, the Court of Appeal was unwilling to accept that walking up, down or along a staircase or balcony amounts to occupation of such a structure.

(iv) *AIB Group (UK) plc* v *Turner* [2015] emphasised the need to look at the type of property. The occupier of a cottage in the UK was living semi-permanently in Barbados and was absent from the cottage for significant periods of time. On the facts she had moved to Barbados and was held not to be in occupation of the cottage as a second home.

(b) When must there be actual occupation?

Abbey National Building Society v *Cann* [1990] 1 All ER 1085 (HL)

Facts
Carpets were laid out and furniture moved before completion without the consent of the seller.

Legal principle
In order to bind a purchaser, there must be occupation at the time of the disposition, i.e. completion of the purchase, and here there were only acts preparatory to completion. In addition, where title is registered, the rights must remain subsisting at the time of registration.

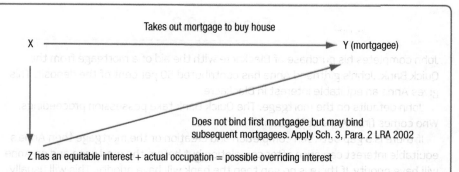

Takes out mortgage to buy house

X ──────────────────────────▶ Y (mortgagee)

Does not bind first mortgagee but may bind subsequent mortgagees. Apply Sch. 3, Para. 2 LRA 2002

Z has an equitable interest + actual occupation = possible overriding interest

Analysis

There is a gap (albeit often short today) between execution of a registrable disposition (e.g. execution of the transfer) and actual registration of the title (the registration gap). This case establishes that actual occupation *at the date of the disposition* is essential.

In *Thompson* v *Foy* (2009) there was actual occupation at the date of the disposition as the claimant's furniture and bedding remained at the house but not at the date of registration as she had then decided that she would not go back to the house to live. It was held *obiter* that the interest must exist at both dates but the other view is that it is enough for the interest to exist at the date of the disposition.

Note that by Schedule 3, Paragraph 2 of the LRA 2002 the overriding interest only extends to land of which the person is in actual occupation: therefore, if they do not occupy the whole of the registered plot they cannot claim an overriding interest over the whole.

Impress your examiner

- -

The recent cases on actual occupation make this a likely subject for exam questions. Read the articles suggested in the 'Key further reading' section at the end of this chapter.

(c) Is there a gap between completion of the purchase and creation of the mortgage? This is often referred to as a *scintilla temporis* (fragment of time) between the two.

Example 2.3

John completes his purchase of Blackacre with the aid of a mortgage from the Quick Bank. John's girlfriend Anne has contributed 50 per cent of the deposit. This gives Anne an equitable interest in Blackacre.

John defaults on the mortgage. The Quick Bank take possession proceedings. Who comes first: Anne or the bank?

If there is a gap between completion and creation of the mortgage then Anne's equitable interest can arise after completion but before the mortgage and so Anne will have priority. If there is no gap then the bank will have priority. This will usually be the case.

In *Abbey National Building Society* v *Cann* [1990] Lord Oliver said: 'In the vast majority of cases the acquisition of the legal estate and the charge are not only precisely simultaneous but indissolubly bound together' and so in this type of case there is no gap. However, in *Scott* v *Southern Pacific Mortgages Limited* [2014] UKSC 52 Lady Hale, with the agreement of Lords Wilson and Reed, held that transactions might not be treated as one, e.g. where the parties to each were not aware of one another's existence, in cases of fraud and in cases where banks had not carried out the appropriate checks. This has opened up an element of uncertainty in this area which had previously been clear, if not always fair.

Impress your examiner

The effect of the decision in *Cann* was to confine the *Boland* principle to cases where there is a gap between completion and the creation of the mortgage, typically second mortgages, and was considered part of the 'retreat from Boland'. Other cases which are said to be examples of this are:

- *City of London Building Society* v *Flegg* (1987): an overriding interest can be overreached.

- *Paddington Building Society* v *Mendelsohn* (1985): occupier may have consented by implication to the mortgage; the principle in this case can often be applied alongside that in *Cann* (above) in an exam.

- *Credit and Mercantile plc* v *Kaymuu* (2015): where a lender's interest did not override the beneficial interest of an occupier where the occupier had left the management of the property entirely in the hands of S, who had arranged the mortgage without the occupier's knowledge or consent. This goes much further than *Paddington* (above).

- *Equity and Law Home Loans Ltd* v *Prestidge* (1992): a person who consents to a mortgage is deemed to consent to a later mortgage which replaces it to the extent of the amount secured by the first mortgage plus interest. This applies even if the person did not know of the replacement mortgage.
- *Hypo Mortgage Services Ltd* v *Robinson* (1997): a child cannot be in actual occupation, for the reason that, otherwise, the interests of lenders on mortgages could be defeated by conferring a (possibly very small) interest on a minor.

Baker v *Craggs* (2016) EWCA 3250 (Ch) (HC)

Facts

Mr and Mrs X sold part of their farm (Blackacre) comprising fields, barns and an adjacent yard to Y. Y could not register his title at once as a plan was incomplete but he visited the land almost daily and carried out work on a barn.

Mr and Mrs X then sold some other land (Whiteacre) to Z which included a right of way (legal easement) over the land sold to Y but as yet unregistered by Y.

Was Y bound by Z's easement?

Legal principle

The purported grant of the easement over Blackacre by X to Z could not prevail over Y's right to be registered as the proprietor of Blackacre free from the easement, because Y's equitable interest in Blackacre under the bare trust arising on completion of his purchase was protected by his actual occupation of Blackacre, and was therefore an overriding interest under section 29 of the LRA 2002 and Schedule 3, Paragraph 2 to LRA 2002. This right could not be defeated by the subsequent grant of the easement to Z. ▶

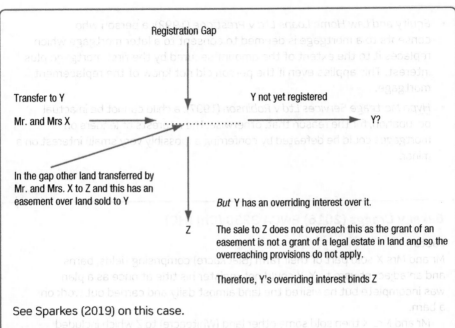

Registration Gap

Transfer to Y   Y not yet registered

Mr. and Mrs X ⟶ .... ⟶ Y?

In the gap other land transferred by
Mr. and Mrs. X to Z and this has an
easement over land sold to Y

But Y has an overriding interest over it.

Z   The sale to Z does not overreach this as the grant of an
         easement is not a grant of a legal estate in land and so the
         overreaching provisions do not apply.

Therefore, Y's overriding interest binds Z

See Sparkes (2019) on this case.

Analysis
The HC had held that Y's rights were overreached on the sale to Z but the CA held
that this was wrong: section 2(1) of the LPA 1925 (the overreaching provision)
applied only upon a conveyance to a purchaser of a *legal estate in land*, and an
easement was not a 'legal estate in land'. Instead the question was simply one of
priority and Y's rights had priority over Z's.

Check Chapter 1 for the principle of overreaching. Note the decision in *Shami* v
Shami (2012) that even where the sale is by one owner, beneficial interests can be
overreached where no capital money arises on the sale. Dixon (2013) 'Editorial:
Reaching up for the box in the attic' 77 *Conv*. 165 points out that, as a result, in a *Boland*
type of case the sole owner could ensure that the beneficial interests were overreached
simply by taking the charge and arranging for payment of the loan to occur later, or
through an overdraft.

Impress your examiner

One way of looking at the cases in this area, which is very useful for essays, is to
ask if they represent a 'retreat from *Boland*', i.e. given that *Boland* gave priority to
the interests of mortgagees, do subsequent cases do so?

Exam tip

In an essay question where you are discussing the position of lenders, you could make a link with the law on undue influence, especially as recent cases have involved this. As explained in Chapter 9, in *Royal Bank of Scotland plc* v *Etridge (No. 2)* (2001), the HL decided that provided that a lender follows certain steps then the loan made will not be affected by the undue influence of another. Thus, here also there is greater protection for lenders than before.

See *Bank of Baroda* v *Dhillon* (1998) (Chapter 3). If a mortgagee applies for a sale under section 14(1) of the Trusts of Land and Appointment of Trustees Act 1996 (TLATA) rather than under the mortgagee's own power of sale, this will in effect override an overriding interest. It may be, however, as in this case, that the occupier, as a beneficiary under a trust, will be entitled to first payment out of the proceeds of sale. This could be a neat way to round off an answer to a problem question.

Easements and profits

- Legal easements and profits created expressly on or after 13 October 2003 (i.e. by deed) are registrable dispositions.
- Equitable easements and profits created on or after 13 October 2003 must be registered to bind a purchaser.
- The only new legal easements and profits that can be overriding are those:

    (a) created by implied reservation;

    (b) created by implied grant (rule in *Wheeldon* v *Burrows* (1879) or s. 62(1), LPA 1925);

    (c) created by prescription (Sch. 3, Para. 3, LRA 2002).

Where an easement can be overriding, it will be in exactly the same way as for rights of occupiers (see Sch. 3, Para. 2, above) but there is one extra point to remember:

Where the person entitled to the easement or profit proves that it has been exercised in the year previous to the disposition, then it will in effect always be overriding.

Example 2.4

X has a right of way (easement) over Y's land. Y sells the land to Z.

- If the easement was granted by deed, it will not bind Z unless registered.
- If the easement was granted by agreement but not in a deed, it is equitable and will not bind Z unless protected on the register.

▶

- If the easement was created by implied reservation, implied grant or prescription, it can be overriding as it may bind Z where cases (i) or (ii) in Schedule 3, Paragraph 3 (above) apply. However, it will bind Z if X exercised it in the year previous to the disposition (sale to Z).

Impress your examiner

This whole area, and particularly overriding interests, is a very likely one for an essay question. Read the articles suggested in the 'Key further reading' section at the end of this chapter.

Local land charges

You will not get a detailed question on these in the exam but you should know what they are. They are not the same as land charges in unregistered land (see below) and are contained in a register maintained by district (or unitary) councils, e.g. compulsory purchase orders, tree preservation orders.

Transitional provisions

- Legal leases which were overriding before 13 October 2003 (i.e. legal leases granted for up to 21 years) remain so.
- Legal and equitable easements and profits which were overriding before 13 October 2003 remain so.
- Interests which ceased to be overriding in 2013, e.g. franchise (right to hold a market) and liability to repair the chancel of a church: holders of these interests had until then to register them. The Chancel Repair Bill (2015) proposed the abolition of chancel repair liability on the basis that the registration period has now expired, but this did not become law. If chancel repair liability is ever abolished, it will make academic the decision in *Aston Cantlow PCC* v *Wallbank* (2003) where the HL rejected a claim that such liability was in breach of the Human Rights Act 1998.

Overriding interests that are abolished by the LRA 2002, i.e. do not override under either first or subsequent registration, are:

- Rights acquired or in the course of acquisition under the Limitation Acts – because of new rules for acquiring title here. See Chapter 10.

Impress your examiner

The existence of overriding interests has been criticised and you should be prepared for an essay question asking you whether they can be justified. The following reasons are put forward to justify their continued existence. Look at them and then read further to expand these points.

- They can easily be discovered by a purchaser.
- The value which is protected by the overriding interest is greater than the value of having all interests registered.
- It is not worth putting some interests on the register.

Protected registered interests

These were formerly known as minor interests. **Protected registered interests** are interests in land which are neither registrable dispositions nor overriding interests and include: covenants on freehold land; equitable easements and profits; estate contracts.

There is no catalogue of these interests in the LRA 2002: essentially they are interests which do not fall within the other two categories.

Most of these must be protected by an entry on the register to bind a purchaser. Note one significant change from the pre-LRA 2002 law: where an overriding interest is protected on the register by a notice, it ceases to be an overriding interest even if the notice is later removed from the register (s. 29(3), LRA).

There are two ways in which an interest can be protected:

- **By a notice.** This can either be entered with the consent of the registered proprietor (RP) or unilaterally. If it is the latter, the RP can object and the Registrar decides the validity of the claim. Entry on the register does not mean that the interest is recognised by the law as valid; it simply means that it has priority over other interests (s. 32(3) LRA 2002). Certain interests cannot be protected by the entry of a notice: e.g. leases for less than three years, interests under a trust of land and leasehold covenants (s. 33 LRA 2002).

Don't be tempted to . . .

Be sure that you check the possibility that a right may be *both* a protected registered interest and an overriding interest.

Example 2.5

An equitable lease is a protected registered interest, but if the lessee is in actual occupation, he or she may have an overriding interest.

Example 2.6

John agrees with Jane that she shall have a lease of Blackacre. This is an equitable lease and is a protected registrable interest. Jane then goes into occupation under the lease. She now has an overriding interest as a person in actual occupation.

- **By a restriction.** Section 44(1) of the LRA provides that where two or more persons are registered as proprietors, a restriction must be entered to ensure that interests capable of being overreached, in fact are overreached. This applies where the beneficial interest is held under a tenancy in common as the beneficial interest is held in separate shares, but not where it is held under a joint tenancy where the beneficial interest will vest in the surviving joint tenant.

Impress your examiner

Law Commission (1998) Paper 254 envisages the possibility that the courts will still have power to set aside a disposition procured by fraud (see Para. 3.49). It will be interesting to see whether and, if so how, this power is exercised.

The LRA also deals with the law on adverse possession, which is considered in Chapter 10.

Alteration of the register

This is unlikely to appear as a major issue in the exam, but you could mention it in an essay question on how the land registration system works. The rules on when the register can be altered are in section 65 and Schedule 4, LRA 2002.

Indemnities

The principle is that, if it turns out that the register needs to be altered, compensation can be paid to whoever has suffered loss. The details are in section 103 and Schedule 8, LRA 2002.

Unregistered title to land

Meaning of 'unregistered title to land'

This term simply means that the title to the land itself has not been registered, unlike in registered land. Therefore, when buying and selling the land, it is necessary to rely on an examination of the title deeds to the property and make other enquiries rather than having the register to rely on.

However, this does not mean that there is no system of registration at all. Instead, some rights must be registered as land charges but, as the actual title to the land is not registered, they are registered against the name of the estate owner, i.e. the owner of the legal estate of freehold or leasehold.

Do check that you understand this point and, above all, do not confuse registration of land charges with land registration itself.

Rights which must be registered as land charges

There are two crucial points about the land charges scheme which you must remember for your exam:

- A registered land charge is automatically binding on a purchaser: the fact that a purchaser has no notice of it is irrelevant. The purchaser is expected to check the land charges register.
- If a land charge is not registered, it will not be binding on a purchaser, even if he/she does have notice.

To sum up: the only thing that matters is whether the right was registered as a land charge.

What rights must be registered as land charges?

Under the Land Charges Act 1925 (now the Land Charges Act 1972) a system was introduced under which the rights registrable as land charges are classified under the headings of A, B, C, D, E and F. They are set out in section 2 of the 1972 Act.

The ones to remember for the exam are:

Class C(i): puisne mortgage – i.e. a second or subsequent mortgage. These are legal mortgages which are not protected by the deposit of the title deeds to the property as the first mortgagee will have these. These are the only legal interests that are registrable as land charges.

Class C(iv): an estate contract. These include contracts to buy the fee simple and also contracts for a lease – equitable leases (see Chapter 6).

Class D(ii): a restrictive covenant entered into on or after 1 January 1926.

Class D(iii): an equitable easement or profit created or arising on or after 1 January 1926.

You should learn the parts in *italic* very carefully.

In addition, the exam may require a knowledge of a *Class F Land Charge*. Under the Family Law Act 1996, spouses and (since the Civil Partnerships Act 2004) civil partners have a personal right of occupation of the family home and this can be enforced against a purchaser if registered. Note that this is a personal right and does not give the spouse or civil partner an interest in the land.

Consequences of non-registration

Section 4, Land Charges Act 1972

Land charges in categories C(i) and F are void against a purchaser of any interest in the land (s. 4(5)).

Land charges in the other categories, C(iv), D(ii) and D(iii), are void only against a purchaser for money or money's worth (s. 4(6)).

Section 199(1)(i), Law of Property Act 1925

If a right is capable of registration as a land charge but is not so registered, then a purchaser is not prejudicially affected by notice of it. The effect is that a purchaser is not bound by it.

See *Midland Bank Trust Co. Ltd* v *Green* (1981) for an illustration of this principle and contrast *Lloyds Bank* v *Carrick* (1996), where, although an estate contract was not registered as a land charge, it could still bind a purchaser as the contract created a trust or, alternatively, an estoppel.

Impress your examiner

Improve your exam marks by reading the judgment of Lord Wilberforce in the HL in *Midland Bank Trust Co. Ltd* v *Green* (1981) and contrasting the approach of Denning MR in the CA who argued that there was a constructive trust in favour of the son which bound the bank. Although Denning MR's argument failed, there are echoes of it in *Lloyds Bank* v *Carrick* (1996). See above under registered land for the proposal in Law Commission Paper 254, which envisages that the courts will still have power to set aside a disposition procured by fraud, and look at the much criticised registered land case of *Peffer* v *Rigg* (1978).

Rights which are not registrable as land charges

Exam tip

You must be absolutely clear for the exam if a right is registrable as a land charge. If it is, then check the rules above on the consequences of non-registration.

If not, then we ask if it is:

- a legal interest? If so, it is binding on a purchaser automatically.
- an equitable interest? If so, whether it is binding depends on whether the purchaser was a bona fide purchaser for value without notice.

Equitable interests

What does bona fide purchaser for value without notice mean?

Bona fide means that the purchaser must be in good faith. It may mean that a person who buys for an improper purpose would not be protected, but see *Midland Bank* v *Green* (discussed earlier).

Purchaser for value means that some value must be given and this includes money, money's worth and marriage. A donee (who takes by gift) would not take free of an equitable interest.

Notice. This is the most important requirement. **Notice** means any of the following:

- Actual notice, i.e. actual knowledge.
- Constructive notice. This has two elements:

  (i) A purchaser is bound by any matters which would be revealed by an examination of the deeds. As a result of this rule, it is common for a note of equitable interests to be made on the back of deeds.

  (ii) A purchaser is bound by all matters which would be revealed by an inspection of the land (rule in *Hunt* v *Luck* (1901)).

- Imputed notice. This means that a purchaser has notice of any matters of which his agent has notice, as in *Kingsnorth Finance Co. Ltd* v *Tizard* (1986), where the mortgagee was bound by the knowledge of the surveyor.

Don't be tempted to . . .

Don't assume that you need to come to a definite conclusion on whether a purchaser had notice (especially constructive notice) or not. What is vital is to state the rules clearly and apply them to the facts as far as you can.

Don't be tempted to . . .

Don't forget that overriding interests *only* arise where title to the land is registered.

One way to look at rights where title is unregistered is to divide them into family interests under trusts which are often overreached as in *Flegg* but otherwise are subject to the doctrine of notice, and commercial interests, e.g. easements. These must be registered as land charges but note that one legal interest is also registrable as a land charge – see below.

Go through the following table and make sure that you can remember where each right fits in. I am afraid that this is just hard slog!

Interest	Registrable as a land charge?
Legal easements and profits	No: they are legal interests and bind a purchaser automatically
Interests of a beneficiary under a trust	No: they are equitable interests and so whether they bind a bona fide purchaser depends on notice
Equitable easements and profits (post-1926)	Yes
Equitable easements and profits (pre-1926)	No: they are equitable interests and so whether they bind a bona fide purchaser depends on notice
Restrictive covenants (post-1926)	Yes
Restrictive covenants (pre-1926)	No: they are equitable interests and so whether they bind a bona fide purchaser depends on notice
Estate contracts	Yes
Puisne mortgages	Yes. N.B. these are the only legal interests in this table to require protection as land charges

Don't be tempted to . . .

Students often fail to go through problem questions in this area logically. Make sure that you first go to this table and then follow through the consequences of the right being legal or equitable and if it is registrable as a land charge or not. Make sure that you do this.

Putting it all together

Sample question

Could you answer this question? Below is a typical problem question which could arise on this topic. Additionally, a sample essay question and guidance on tackling it can be found on the companion website.

Problem question

John has bought a registered freehold house with some farmland from Steve.

After John's purchase, Fred, Susie and Jean, who are all neighbours, come to see him with letters signed by Steve.

Fred has a letter granting him the right to cut wood from trees on the land.

Susie has a letter agreeing to grant her a lease of one acre of the farmland. Susie has not started to use the land.

Jean has a letter stating that she has a licence to park her caravan on the land.

In addition, Elsie, Steve's mother arrives and says that she paid half the purchase price when Steve bought the house and so she has a right to stay there. Elsie was away on holiday when John purchased the house.

Advise John on whether he is bound by any of these claims. How would your answer differ if title was unregistered?

Answer guidelines

Approaching the question

This is the very type of question where a calm logical approach in the exam will pay great dividends!

- You must first *identify* the interest: is it legal or equitable? (This also helps when you come to unregistered title.)
- Then *decide* where it fits in the registration of title to land scheme.
- Then adopt the same approach for unregistered land.

Important points to include

Assuming that title is registered

- *Fred*: equitable profit – needs to be protected by a notice on the register. If not, not binding.
- *Susie*: equitable lease – same as for Fred but if she had actually started to use the land she could claim that she had an overriding interest as a person in occupation under her equitable lease.

- *Jean:* no right to register – just a personal right.
- *Elsie:* may have an overriding interest as a person in actual occupation.

Assuming that title is unregistered

Do the interests need to be registered as land charges?

- *Fred's* profit – yes.
- *Susie's* equitable lease – yes – as an estate contract.
- *Jean's* licence – no – not a proprietary right.
- *Elsie's* right under a trust – no. However, Elsie's right, unlike Jean's, is a proprietary right. As it is equitable, whether or not John is bound depends on whether he has notice – apply *Kingsnorth Finance Co. Ltd* v *Tizard.*

Impress your examiner

Good knowledge of the relevant case law, especially in relation to Elsie and cases on what is meant by actual occupation. State that even if Elsie does have an overriding interest, John may not be bound by it – apply Schedule 3, Paragraph 2, LRA 2002. You can also make mention of *Bank of Baroda* v *Dhillon* re Elsie (see Chapter 3).

Key case summary

Key case	How to use	Related topics
Williams & Glyn's Bank v *Boland*	To show how an overriding interest can arise through acquisition of an interest in land coupled with occupation.	Beneficial interests in land.
Abbey National Building Society v *Cann*	To explain, in an answer on overriding interests of occupiers, exactly when there must be occupation to bind a purchaser.	Overriding interests.
Baker v *Craggs*	To explain the interaction between the rules on priority, overriding interests and overreaching.	Registered land.

Key further reading

Key articles/reports	How to use	Related topics
Sparkes, P. (2019) Overreaching, trust breaking and underreaching. 1 *Conv.* 14.	In contrast to other commentators, who have been critical of the HC decision in *Baker* v *Craggs*, this article argues that it has some merit. This different view is valuable. Contrast it with that of Dixon (below).	Overriding interests and overreaching.
Bogusz, B. (2014) The relevance of intention and wishes to determine actual occupation: a sea change in judicial thinking? 78 *Conv.* 27.	This is especially useful on the case law on actual occupation.	Meaning of occupation under the LRA 2002. Schedule 3.
Bevan. C (2016) Overriding and over-extended? Actual occupation: a call to orthodoxy. 2 *Conv.* 104.	This has a different perspective on the cases on the meaning of occupation under the LRA 2002 and argues that in the cases little or no reference has been made to the broader aims of land registration or the legislative purpose behind the provisions being applied.	
Dixon, M. (2017) The registration gap and overreaching. 1 *Conv.* 1.	This article is useful to read alongside that of Sparkes (above) as it is critical of the HC decision in *Baker* v *Craggs*.	Overriding interests and overreaching.

Key articles/reports	How to use	Related topics
Law Commission (2001) Paper 271, Land registration for the 21st century – a conveyancing revolution.	It was this report which led to the passage of the LRA 2002 and for a really good mark in your exams you really do need to be familiar with the thinking behind it.	Land Registration.

go.pearson.com/uk/lawexpress

Go online to access more revision support including quizzes to test your knowledge, sample questions with answer guidelines, printable versions of the topic maps, and more!

3

Co-ownership of land

Revision checklist

Essential points you should know:

- Features of a joint tenancy and a tenancy in common
- How a joint tenancy can be severed
- Powers of trustees of land
- Rights of beneficiaries to occupy
- Who can apply for sale of the land and principles on which the court orders a sale

Topic map

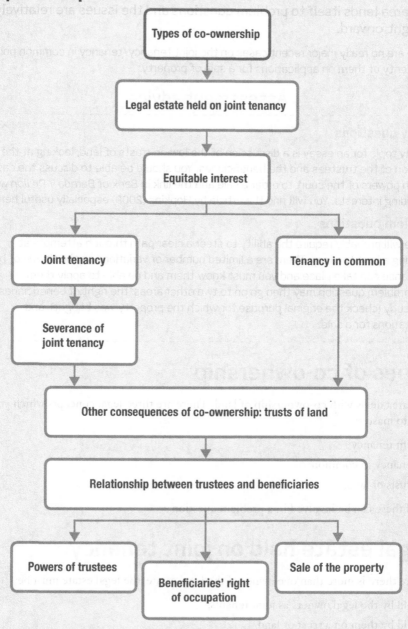

Types of co-ownership

Legal estate held on joint tenancy

Equitable interest

Joint tenancy

Tenancy in common

Severance of joint tenancy

Other consequences of co-ownership: trusts of land

Relationship between trustees and beneficiaries

Powers of trustees

Beneficiaries' right of occupation

Sale of the property

A printable version of this topic map is available from **go.pearson.com/uk/lawexpress**

Introduction

This area lends itself to problem questions and the issues are relatively straightforward.

There are no really major recent cases on the joint tenancy/tenancy in common point but plenty of them on applications for a sale of property.

Assessment advice

Essay questions

A likely topic for an essay is a discussion of the law on trusts of land, looking at the position of the trustees and the beneficiaries. You should be able to discuss the case law on powers of the court to order a sale and the link in *Bank of Baroda* v *Dhillon* with overriding interests. You will find the article by Hopkins (2009) especially useful here.

Problem questions

These will probably require the ability to steer a clear path through attempts at severing a joint tenancy. There are a limited number of variations on the theme of how severance can take place and you must know them and be able to apply them.

A problem question may then go on to two other areas: the right of beneficiaries to occupy (check the original purpose for which the property was bought), and applications for a sale.

Types of co-ownership

This area deals with co-ownership of land. There are three legal concepts which you need to master:

- Joint tenancy
- Tenancy in common
- Trusts of land.

All of these can be involved in a problem question.

Legal estate held on joint tenancy

Where there is more than one owner of the legal estate, the legal estate must be:

- held by the legal owners as joint tenants;
- held by them on a trust of land.

Four unities are necessary for a **joint tenancy** to exist:

- Time: the interests of all must vest at the same time.
- Title: all must derive their title from the same document.
- Interest: all must have the same interest.
- Possession: all must be equally entitled to possession of the whole land.

Joint tenancy exists where there are no shares, i.e. all the joint tenants own all the land jointly and the four unities are present.

Two vital points:

(1) Co-owners cannot hold the legal estate as **tenants in common**.
(**Tenancy in common** exists where the beneficial owners have shares in the land.)

(2) The distinguishing feature of joint tenancy is the right of survivorship: as joint tenants own no individual share, they cannot leave any part of their joint tenancy by will, nor does it pass under the intestacy rules. Instead it passes to the surviving joint tenants. Section 184 of the LPA 1925 provides that where deaths occur in circumstances making it uncertain which died first, then the younger shall be deemed to have survived the elder (see *Hickman* v *Peacey* (1945) – deaths in a bomb blast). Note also the recent case of *Scarle* v *Scarle* (2019) where a married couple had been found dead in their home and it was held that as the order of deaths was uncertain section 184 operated to create a presumption that the wife, being the younger of the two, had survived her husband for succession purposes.

Example 3.1

The legal estate to Blackacre is held by X and Y. This means that:

- they are joint tenants;
- there is a trust of land.

X dies. The legal estate automatically vests in Y only.

Note that survivorship can also apply to tenancies held jointly. See Loveland (2015) on the problems this can cause and on whether Article 8 of the ECHR is engaged as illustrated by *Solihull MBC* v *Hickin* (2012).

Number of joint tenants

> ## Section 34(2), Law of Property Act 1925
>
> Where land is conveyed to co-owners who are of full age they:
> - must be joint tenants;
> - cannot be more than four.

Exam tip

You often find that there are more than four persons named in the question. If so:

- if they are all of full age, the first four take the legal estate but they can all take an equitable (beneficial) interest – see section immediately following this box;
- if any of them are under 18, then they drop out and only have a beneficial interest.

Equitable interest

Here there is a choice: it can be held on either:

- joint tenancy; or
- tenancy in common.

Joint tenancy

This means that the right of survivorship applies to the beneficial interest.

Tenancy in common

This is the opposite of a joint tenancy. The only unity required is possession. Each is entitled to a separate undivided share and can dispose of this share either during life or on death. Sometimes the four unities are present, but there are words of severance and, therefore, there is a tenancy in common.

Remember that in a tenancy in common:

- there are separate shares;
- the right of survivorship does not apply.

Example 3.2

X and Y hold the legal estate in Blackacre on trust for themselves and Z.
- The legal title must be held on a joint tenancy.
- The equitable interest can be held on either a joint tenancy or a tenancy in common.

If the equitable interest is held on a tenancy in common, X, Y and Z each have a separate share, which they can sell or which can devolve on their death.

How do we tell if there is a joint tenancy or a tenancy in common?

The question may make it clear.

Example 3.3

X and Y agree that if they die their interest in the property shall go to the other.

This agreement overrides anything else such as unequal contributions to the purchase price (see 'Presumptions of equity' later), and there will be a joint tenancy as the parties intend that the right of survivorship shall apply.

The question may not make it clear and so you must look for:

Words of severance

Even if the four unities exist there will not be a joint tenancy if there are words of **severance**, i.e. words which indicate that the parties are to hold separate shares. Examples are:

- 'in equal shares': *Payne* v *Webb* (1874);
- 'equally': *Lewen* v *Dodd* (1595);
- 'to be divided between': *Peat* v *Chapman* (1750).

Presumptions of equity

If there are no words of severance, then look at this:

Equity leans against a joint tenancy and the law leans against a tenancy in common. In the following cases equity presumes that there is a tenancy in common:

- Purchase in unequal shares: *Lake* v *Gibson* (1729); *Bull* v *Bull* (1955).
- Where there is a relationship of a commercial character, e.g. partnership property: *Re Fuller* (1933).

- Where money is lent on mortgage by two or more persons, they are presumed to hold the estate which they receive by way of security as tenants in common: *Morley* v *Bird* (1798).

Remember: if there is an express agreement that the parties will hold as joint tenants, this will override any of the above presumptions.

Exam tip

Always refer to a joint tenant as having an interest, but a tenant in common as having a share.

Severance of joint tenancy

Severance of an equitable joint tenancy to turn it into a tenancy in common

Exam tip

Problem questions frequently require you to look at this area. As a useful guide, the situation in the question usually involves a joint tenancy as it can be severed.

Section 3(4), Administration of Estates Act 1925

Severance cannot be effected by will.

There are two ways to sever a joint tenancy:

- by notice in writing;
- in equity.

Severance by notice in writing

Section 36(2), Law of Property Act 1925

A joint tenant may give notice of intention to sever to all other joint tenants.

Any notice must be in writing (s. 196(1), LPA 1925) and giving notice means serving notice (s. 196(3) and (4), LPA 1925).

See *Re 88 Berkeley Road* (1971) and *Kinch* v *Bullard* (1999).

Severance in equity

'**Severance in equity** may be defined as such acts or things as would, in the case of personal estate, sever the tenancy in equity' (*Williams* v *Hensman* (1861)).

In *Williams* v *Hensman* (1861) Page-Wood VC said that there are three methods:

(1) An act of any one of the parties operating on his own share, e.g. a sale of the joint tenant's beneficial interest or the bankruptcy of a joint tenant. In equity a sale will take place as soon as there is a specifically enforceable contract to sell.

Example 3.4

- -

X sells his beneficial interest in Blackacre to W. This severs X's interest in equity and so W is a tenant in common.

Don't be tempted to . . .

- -

Students often think that when an equitable joint tenant sells his interest he also ceases to be a holder of the legal estate. This is wrong – it is unaffected. So, in Example 3.4, X will only cease to hold the legal estate if there is a transfer to the other joint tenants.

(2) Mutual agreement. In *Burgess* v *Rawnsley* (1975) an oral agreement by one joint tenant to purchase the share of the other operated to sever even though the contract was not specifically enforceable as there was nothing in writing. See also *Hunter* v *Babbage* (1994).

(3) Any other course of dealing, which shows that the interests of all were mutually treated as constituting a tenancy in common. In *Burgess* Sir John Pennycuick said that it includes negotiations which, although not resulting in an agreement, indicate a common intention to sever. Denning MR said that it included a course of dealing in which one party makes it clear to the others that he 'desires that their shares should no longer be held jointly but be held in common', but Pennycuick's view seems to represent the law. Boost your marks in an answer on this point by referring to Alvin W-L S. (2019) on different decisions of the Singapore courts on this area.

Don't be tempted to . . .

- -

Students often overlook that any agreement or common intention must be between all of the co-owners. This is a common examination point. Check the question carefully to see if this is so.

Forfeiture

If one joint tenant kills another, the right of survivorship should not operate, as this would allow the murderer to benefit from his act.

See Chapter 4 and especially *Stack* v *Dowden* and *Jones* v *Kernott*, for the law on deciding beneficial interests in the family home where the legal title is held as joint tenants.

Other consequences of co-ownership: trust of land

Trusts of land

Once the question of who holds the legal title has been dealt with, one can then turn to the question of the terms on which it is held. The answer is that under the Trusts of Land and Appointment of Trustees Act 1996 (TLATA), a trust of land automatically comes into existence whenever the legal title to land is held by joint tenants (s. 36(1), LPA, as amended by the TLATA).

Note that until TLATA came into force, land held on trust was held on a trust for sale.

The following are the main provisions of the TLATA and all references to sections are to sections of that Act.

Exam tip

In an exam, you will need to be able to apply these statutory provisions. It is essential that you know what area each section deals with and how they relate to each other.

Relationship between trustees and beneficiaries

Powers of trustees

Trustees have all the powers of an absolute owner of land (s. 6(1) TLATA) but, as trustees, they are bound by the fiduciary duties of trustees when exercising their functions. As Megarry VC put it in *Cowan* v *Scargill* (1984): 'they must put the interests of the beneficiaries first'.

Section 6, Trusts of Land and Appointment of Trustees Act 1996

Confers two specific powers of trustees:

(a) to purchase land by way of investment for the occupation of any beneficiary or for any other reason;

(b) to transfer the land to the beneficiaries when they are all of full age and capacity even though they have not requested this.

Exclusion and restriction of powers

Section 8(1), Trusts of Land and Appointment of Trustees Act 1996

This allows the settlor to exclude all or any of the provisions of section 6.

Delegation by trustees

Section 9, Trusts of Land and Appointment of Trustees Act 1996

This provides that the trustees may, by power of attorney, delegate any of their functions relating to land to a beneficiary of full age and capacity who is entitled to an interest in possession in land. Any delegation must be unanimous and, therefore, only one trustee is needed to revoke it as this destroys unanimity. If trustees refuse to delegate, an application may be made to the court under section 14 by a beneficiary for an order that a delegation should be made. Any delegate beneficiary has the same duties as an actual trustee.

Consultation with beneficiaries

Section 11(1), Trusts of Land and Appointment of Trustees Act 1996

This provides that trustees must 'so far as practicable' consult the beneficiaries of full age who are beneficially entitled to an interest in possession in the land and 'so far as is consistent with the general interest of the trust' to give effect to those wishes or, in cases of dispute, the wishes of the majority, according to the value of their combined interests.

Beneficiaries' rights of occupation

Section 12, Trusts of Land and Appointment of Trustees Act 1996

This gives a right of occupation to beneficiaries who are entitled to an interest in possession in the land, provided that the trust so allows, but no right of occupation arises if the land is either unavailable or unsuitable for occupation by the beneficiary in question.

Section 13, Trusts of Land and Appointment of Trustees Act 1996

This allows the trustees power to exclude or restrict the right to occupy, but the power must not be exercised unreasonably. Conditions may be imposed on occupation and section 13(5) sets out examples: paying outgoings and complying with obligations, e.g. ensuring that any planning permission is complied with. Section 13(4) sets out matters to which the trustees must have regard when exercising their powers to restrict or exclude the right to occupy: intentions of the settlor, purposes for which the land is held on trust; and the circumstances and wishes of beneficiaries who would be entitled to occupy but for the exclusion or restriction. Section 13(7) provides that a person in occupation of the land, whether or not in occupation under section 12, shall not be evicted except with their consent or a court order. This includes those in occupation under other rights than those of a trust beneficiary, e.g. a matrimonial home right under the Family Law Act 1996. The court, when deciding whether to evict, may, by section 13(8), have regard to the matters set out in section 13(4).

Sale of the property

Powers of the court to order a sale

These are contained in the following sections: section 14 deals with who can apply and section 15 with the principles on which the court can order a sale.

Section 14, Trusts of Land and Appointment of Trustees Act 1996

This allows any person interested in the trust to apply to the court for an order, which could, e.g., be for a sale (see below), or authorising what would otherwise be a breach of trust. The term 'any person interested' includes trustees, beneficiaries, remaindermen and secured creditors of beneficiaries.

Section 15(1), Trusts of Land and Appointment of Trustees Act 1996

This sets out the following criteria to which the courts must have regard when settling disputes:

(a) the intentions of the settlor;

(b) the purposes for which the property is held on trust;

(c) the welfare of any minor who either occupies, or might reasonably be expected to occupy, the land as his home;

(d) the interests of any secured creditor of any beneficiary.

Note that (d) will only apply where the secured creditor is *not* a mortgagee who has priority over the other creditors. If the mortgagee does have priority then it can sell under its power of sale – see Chapter 9.

In practice, and certainly in examination questions, these criteria are particularly relevant when looking at disputes over whether land should be sold.

Bank of Ireland Home Mortgages Ltd v *Bell* [2001] 2 All ER (Comm) 920 (CA)

Facts

The family home was owned jointly by the husband (H) and wife (W) in law but the wife had only a 10 per cent beneficial interest. H forged W's signature on a mortgage and then left W. She remained in the house with their son for 10 years after H stopped making mortgage repayments, and when the bank sought possession W was in poor health.

Legal principle

The mortgage debt was now £300,000 and a sale would be ordered, as a 'powerful consideration' was 'whether the creditor is receiving proper recompense for being kept out of his money'. This was clearly not the case.

Analysis

Compare this case with the earlier one of *Mortgage Corporation* v *Shaire* (2001), where Neuberger J said that: 'By comparison with the previous law' (i.e. in the LPA 1925), Parliament had intended to 'tip the scales more in favour of families and against banks and other chargees'.

Bank of Baroda v *Dhillon* [1998] 1 FLR 524 (HC)

Facts

A bank applied for an order for sale of the matrimonial home.

Legal principle

This would be granted even though the wife had an overriding interest under the LRA 1925 (now Sch. 3, Para. 2, LRA 2002) which bound the bank. The crucial factor was that the children were grown up and, after the sale, W would still have enough money for other accommodation.

Analysis

This case shows that even where an occupier has an overriding interest (see Chapter 2) this may be overridden by the court in granting a sale of the property. Although this case was decided under the previous law (s. 30, LPA 1925) there is no reason to think that the decision would differ under sections 14 and 15, TLATA.

An early case on section 30, LPA, which is probably still good law is *Re Buchanan-Wollaston's Conveyance* (1939). Here, land was bought by four co-owners to prevent it from being built on. One later wished to sell but the others did not. As the original purpose remained, the court refused to order a sale. Note *Baxter* v *Stancomb* (2018) on the relationship between subsections 15(1)(a) and (b). Here the intentions of the parties (ground (a)) were usefully contrasted with the purposes of the trust (ground (b)) – see paras 56-65 of the judgment.

Read *Barca* v *Mears* (2004) on the relationship between sections 14 and 15, TLATA, and the Human Rights Act (Art. 8 – respect for private and family life).

Impress your examiner

Read Dixon (2015) who examines *Begum* v *Issa* (2014) where the contest was not, as is usual, between a beneficiary under a trust and a lender but between a beneficiary and a purchaser who wanted to use the property for their own benefit. This will give an extra dimension to your answer.

Putting it all together

Sample question

Could you answer this question? Below is a typical problem question which could arise on this topic. Additionally, a sample essay question and guidance on tackling it can be found on the companion website.

Problem question

In 2017 John, Mark, Conchetta and Louise were students at Melchester University and had won a prize in the lottery. They used their winnings to buy a house for them all to live in while they completed their studies. The purchase price was £200,000.

John contributed £80,000 and the others each paid £40,000. They agreed that the house should belong to them equally and it was registered in the names of them all with a declaration that the survivor could give a receipt for capital money.

Later that year John, having failed to submit an assignment on time, had to leave his course and so he sold his interest in the house to Alf, a fellow student.

Mark got married at Christmas and made a will leaving all his property to his wife Florrie. They went on honeymoon to the seaside but Mark was drowned by a freak wave.

Louise told Conchetta that she could not stand living in the house just with her any longer and that she wanted to sell her share. Conchetta was upset by this and a violent quarrel ensued. Louise then went to her solicitor and, acting on his advice, she sent a notice of severance by registered post to Conchetta. When the notice arrived Conchetta was out and so Louise signed for it.

John and Louise now wish to sell the house but Conchetta and Alf wish to stay.

(a) Advise the parties on the devolution of the legal and equitable interests in the property.

(b) Advise Conchetta and Alf on whether they can remain in the house.

(c) Advise John and Louise on whether they can insist on a sale.

Answer guidelines

Approaching the question

- Part (a): apply the rules on joint tenancies and tenancies in common – all that is required is a clear understanding of the law and a logical approach.

- Parts (b) and (c): here, especially in (c), there is scope for discussion of case law and so more chance to earn vital extra marks!

Important points to include

Stage one: John sells his beneficial interest in the house to Alf, a fellow student.

Stage two: Mark gets married and makes a will leaving all his property to Florrie, and is then drowned. Apply section 3(4), Administration of Estates Act 1925.

Stage three: Louise tells Conchetta that she cannot stand living in the house, etc. There is no severance. Rights remain the same.

Stage four: Louise serves notice of severance.

- Part (a): Follow through the situation as above. Note that inequality of contributions does not make them tenants in common in equity, as their agreement plus the declaration at the Land Registry override this. Apply *Burgess* v *Rawnsley* to the need for an agreement between Louise and Conchetta and *Re 88 Berkeley Road* to the receipt of the notice by Louise.

- Part (b): Right to occupy. Apply section 12, TLATA (also section 11 – need for consultation). If Alf has no right to occupy, then section 13 – right can be restricted.

- Part (c): Cannot insist on sale. Apply section 14 (right to apply) and section 15 (principles on which a sale can be ordered).

Impress your examiner

- Mention the possible application of the Human Rights Act.
- Link with overriding interests.
- Discuss in depth the case law on section 15, TLATA.

Key case summary

Key case	How to use	Related topics
Bank of Ireland Home Mortgages Ltd v *Bell*	Application for a sale of land.	Section 15, TLATA 1996.
Bank of Baroda v *Dhillon*	To show how a sale can be ordered under section 15, TLATA even where the person against whom it is ordered has an overriding interest under LRA 2002.	Overriding interests of persons in occupation.

Key further reading

Key articles/reports	How to use	Related topics
Alvin W-L S. (2019) Severance by unilateral declaration: lessons from Singapore. 2 *Conv.* 138.	To add extra depth to an answer on methods of severance.	Trusts of land.
Dixon, M. (2015) A tangled web of priority. 2 *Conv.* 97.	To explain that there are different possible priorities in applications for a sale of land under TLATA – beneficiaries: lenders; beneficiaries: purchasers, etc.	Applications for a sale under TLATA.
Fox, L. (2005) Creditors and the concept of the family home: a functional analysis. 25 *LS* 201.	Looking at the rights of creditors as against others with an interest in the property when the courts are considering whether to order a sale of a family home.	Applications for a sale under TLATA.

Key articles/reports	How to use	Related topics
Hopkins, N. (2009) Regulating trusts of the home: private law and social policy. 125 *LQR* 310.	In a discussion of the powers of the court to order a sale of land under section 14, TLATA.	Sections 14 and 15, TLATA.
Loveland, I. (2015) Analysing the doctrine of survivorship in joint tenancies of people's homes from a human rights perspective. 1 *Conv.* 47.	To include the Human Rights Act angle in a question on severance.	Joint tenancies.

go.pearson.com/uk/lawexpress

Go online to access more revision support including quizzes to test your knowledge, sample questions with answer guidelines, printable versions of the topic maps, and more!

4

Trusts and the home

Revision checklist

Essential points you should know:

- When the law of trusts is relevant to disputes over the home
- Where the law is now
- How the size of the share is determined
- Rights which an equitable interest gives
- Where the law should be going: approaches in other countries, possible changes in English law

Topic map

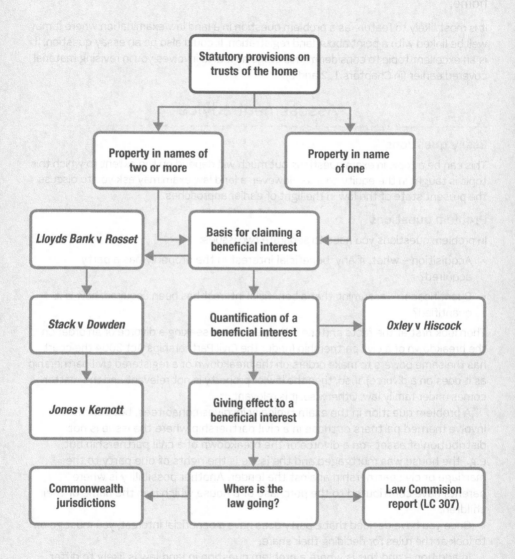

```
                    ┌─────────────────────┐
                    │ Statutory provisions on │
                    │   trusts of the home   │
                    └─────────────────────┘
                         │           │
              ┌──────────┘           └──────────┐
    ┌─────────────────────┐         ┌─────────────────────┐
    │  Property in names of │         │   Property in name   │
    │      two or more      │         │       of one         │
    └─────────────────────┘         └─────────────────────┘
         │          │                        │
┌─────────────────┐  ┌─────────────────────┐
│ Lloyds Bank v   │─▶│   Basis for claiming a │◀─
│    Rosset       │  │   beneficial interest  │
└─────────────────┘  └─────────────────────┘
         │                      │
┌─────────────────┐  ┌─────────────────────┐  ┌─────────────────┐
│  Stack v Dowden │  │   Quantification of a  │─▶│  Oxley v Hiscock │
└─────────────────┘  │   beneficial interest  │  └─────────────────┘
         │           └─────────────────────┘
┌─────────────────┐  ┌─────────────────────┐
│ Jones v Kernott │  │    Giving effect to a  │
└─────────────────┘  │   beneficial interest  │
                     └─────────────────────┘
                                │
┌─────────────────┐  ┌─────────────────────┐  ┌─────────────────┐
│  Commonwealth   │◀─│    Where is the        │─▶│  Law Commision   │
│  jurisdictions  │  │    law going?          │  │  report (LC 307) │
└─────────────────┘  └─────────────────────┘  └─────────────────┘
```

A printable version of this topic map is available from **go.pearson.com/uk/lawexpress**

Introduction

This chapter deals with the part played by equity in disputes over the home.

It is most likely to feature as a problem question in a land law examination where it may well be linked with a point about land registration. It could also be an essay question. It is an excellent topic to consider at this stage as it also involves you in revising material covered earlier (in Chapters 1, 2 and 3).

Assessment advice

Essay questions

This can be a topic in exam questions but much will depend on the extent to which this topic is taught in the equity course. However, a land law exam may ask you to discuss the present state of the law in the light of earlier approaches.

Problem questions

In problem questions you need to separate two issues:

- Acquisition – what, if any, beneficial interest in the property has a party acquired?
- Quantification – assuming that a beneficial interest has been acquired, how is it quantified?

Then look first at the facts and see if the parties are seeking a divorce or an order on the breakdown of a civil partnership (under the Civil Partnerships Act 2004 the court has the same powers to make orders on the breakdown of a registered civil partnership as it does on a divorce). If so, then the law of property is not relevant and the matter comes under family law. Otherwise, it is relevant.

A problem question in the exam typically involves cohabitees, but can involve married partners or those in a civil partnership where the issue is not distribution of assets on a divorce or the breakdown of a civil partnership but, e.g., the house was mortgaged and the issue is the rights of one party to the marriage or civil partnership against the lender. Another possibility is where parents have contributed to the purchase of a house which is in the name of their children.

Once you have decided that a party does have a beneficial interest, you must go on to look at the rules for deciding their share.

In addition – and this is where a problem question in land law is likely to differ from one on this area in an equity exam – the question may also ask you to decide if, assuming that a party does have a beneficial interest in the land, that interest is binding on a purchaser. Here you will need to consider whether title to the land is registered or not (and refer to Chapter 2). You may also need to use the detail in Chapter 3 on the rights contained in the TLATA of beneficiaries and others in land held on trust.

The law of trusts and the home

An exam question often revolves around the following scenario, which involves both this chapter and Chapter 2.

There are two issues:

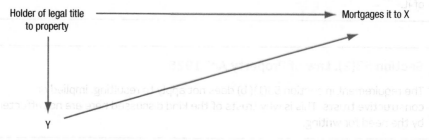

Holder of legal title to property ———————————————→ Mortgages it to X

Y

Claims to have a beneficial interest in the property

- Does Y have a beneficial interest and how is it quantified? This is dealt with in this chapter.
- If Y does have a beneficial interest, then whether X is bound by it will depend on the rules for registered land (Chapter 2 – especially the law on overriding interests) or unregistered land (Chapter 2 – especially the doctrine of notice – see, e.g., *Kingsnorth Finance Co. Ltd* v *Tizard* (1986)).

Exam tip

In any question on this area remember two things:

(a) Ask if this is a case where the legal title to the home is in the name of one party (a sole name case) or both (a joint name case).

(b) Deal with the acquisition issue (does the claimant acquire a beneficial interest at all) separately from the quantification issue (assuming that the claimant has acquired an interest, how is it to be quantified).

First, you need to be aware of the following statutory provisions:

Exam tip

In any problem question you need to point out, near the start of your answer, the relevance of the statutory provisions on the creation of trusts of land.

Section 53(1)(b), Law of Property Act 1925

Declaration of a trust of land must be in writing or there must be written evidence of it.

Section 53(2), Law of Property Act 1925

The requirement in section 53(1)(b) does not apply to resulting, implied or constructive trusts. This is why trusts of the kind discussed here are not affected by the need for writing.

If there is an express declaration of trust which satisfies section 53(1)(b), then this is conclusive unless varied by subsequent agreement or affected by proprietary estoppel (*Goodman* v *Gallant* (1986)).

At the outset of the answer to a problem question, clear the ground and check which of the following applies:

Situation one: Joint name cases. The property is held in the name of two or more persons and the claim concerns the extent of their beneficial shares. If so, the exact ratio of *Stack* v *Dowden* (2007) will apply.

Situation two: Sole name cases. The property is held in the name of one person and the claim is by another person who claims a beneficial interest. If so, although you still need to be aware of the principles stated in *Stack* v *Dowden*, particularly by Lady Hale, and in *Jones* v *Kernott* (2011), the leading case is now *Capehorn* v *Harris* (2015).

Summary of points to consider:

(a) On what basis can a beneficial interest be claimed?

(b) The debate on how the courts decide whether the parties had any common intention regarding the beneficial interests in the property.

(c) The distinction, which is not always made clear by the courts, between the rules for deciding acquisition and quantification of the beneficial interests.

Remember when attempting a family homes question:

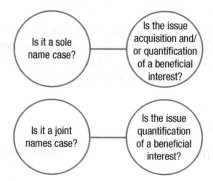

On what basis can a beneficial interest be claimed?

There are three possibilities:

(a) **Resulting trust.** This approach will be most appropriate where the claim is based on contributions to the cost of acquisition of the property and the effect will be that the beneficial shares of the parties will be in proportion to their respective contributions. Some claims to a share in the family home may still be decided on this basis.

(b) **Constructive trust.** This approach will be most appropriate where the claim is based on factors other than, or in addition to, contributions to the cost of acquisition of the property, and the courts, when deciding quantification, can take account of factors other than the cost of acquisition. This is the basis on which claims to a share in the family home are usually decided.

(c) **Proprietary estoppel.** This does not usually arise as a separate issue and is often linked to the imposition of a constructive trust in, e.g., *Lloyds Bank* v *Rosset* (1991) where the estoppel concept of detrimental reliance was used to justify the imposition of a constructive trust. See, however, Gardner (2014) Material relief between ex-cohabitants: otherwise than by beneficial entitlement 3 *Conv.* 202 who suggests that proprietary estoppel might be used to give ancillary relief, especially where the relationship between the parties also involved the claimant working for the defendant, e.g. as a carer or in his business.

The constructive trust approach is the one most often currently used in domestic cases. Check Chapter 5 to revise your knowledge of proprietary estoppel and its relationship to constructive trusts.

Impress your examiner

Note carefully – and point out in the exam – that the present problem with this area of law is that the two cases which lay down fundamental principles (*Stack v Dowden* and *Jones v Kernott*) were where property was held in joint names yet many of the cases are where property is in a sole name.

Development of the case law

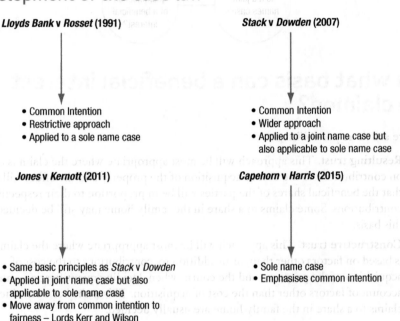

Lloyds Bank v Rosset (1991)

- Common Intention
- Restrictive approach
- Applied to a sole name case

Stack v Dowden (2007)

- Common Intention
- Wider approach
- Applied to a joint name case but also applicable to sole name case

Jones v Kernott (2011)

- Same basic principles as *Stack* v *Dowden*
- Applied in joint name case but also applicable to sole name case
- Move away from common intention to fairness – Lords Kerr and Wilson

Capehorn v Harris (2015)

- Sole name case
- Emphasises common intention

Situation one: joint name cases – the property is held in the names of two or more persons and the claim concerns the extent of their beneficial shares

Stack v Dowden [2007] UKHL 17 (HL)

Facts

The legal title to the house was held as joint tenants. X (the woman) had contributed 65 per cent of the price and the other 35 per cent was provided by a joint loan secured on the legal title held by her and Y (the man). No restriction was entered on the register and the assumption was that they were equitable joint tenants.

Legal principle

Lady Hale held that a conveyance in joint names established a *prima facie* case of a 50:50 split and the burden is on the person seeking to show that the parties did intend their beneficial interests to be different from their legal interests to prove this. This case was unusual in that X had contributed far more to the purchase than Y and, as they had kept their financial affairs rigidly separate, a 65:35 split was justified. The fundamental principle, in Lady Hale's words, is 'to ascertain the parties' shared intentions, actual, inferred or imputed, with respect to the property in the light of their whole course of conduct in relation to it'.

She laid down a number of factors, which she pointed out are not exhaustive, to be considered in deciding this question:

(a) any advice or discussions at the time of the transfer which cast light upon their intentions;

(b) the reasons why the home was acquired in their joint names;

(c) the reasons why (if it be the case) the survivor was authorised to give a receipt for the capital moneys;

(d) the purpose for which the home was acquired;

(e) the nature of the parties' relationship;

(f) whether they had children for whom they both had responsibility to provide a home;

(g) how the purchase was financed, both initially and subsequently;

(h) how the parties arranged their finances, whether separately or together or a bit of both;

(i) how they discharged the outgoings on the property and their other household expenses.

See also Lord Neuberger's judgment in *Laskar* v *Laskar* [2008].

Analysis

The result of *Stack* v *Dowden* is that in cases involving the family home, the presumption of an equitable joint tenancy is very strong and will not usually be rebutted so that there will normally be an equitable joint tenancy even in cases of unequal contributions.

Lord Neuberger dissented and held that the correct approach was a presumption of a resulting trust. This would emphasise the respective contributions of the parties to the purchase price and, on the facts, this would give the same result as that arrived at by Lady Hale but by a different route.

> ### *Jones* v *Kernott* [2011] UKSC 53 (SC)
>
> **Facts**
>
> The parties bought the property in joint names in 1985, with a joint mortgage. They lived there, sharing the household expenses, for over eight years. In 1993 Mr Kernott moved out of the property and made no further contribution towards the acquisition of the property. Ms Jones remained with their two children, paying all the household expenses herself. This continued for over 14 years, when the property was put up for sale.
>
> **Legal principle**
>
> The Supreme Court followed *Stack* v *Dowden* and held that where a property is purchased in the joint names of a married or unmarried couple for joint occupation, who were both responsible for any mortgage, and where there is no express declaration of their beneficial interests, there is a strong presumption that the beneficial interests coincide with the legal estate and so are 50:50.
>
> However, that presumption can be rebutted by evidence of a contrary intention, which might more readily be shown where the parties had contributed to the acquisition of the property in unequal shares, but each case would turn on its own facts. It was for the court to ascertain the parties' common intention as to what their shares in the property would be, in the light of their whole course of conduct in relation to it.
>
> **Analysis**
>
> This decision follows *Stack* v *Dowden* and clarifies its principles. It makes it clear that resulting trust principles will not apply where the family home is purchased in joint names and contributions are unequal.

In *Barnes* v *Phillips* [2015] the CA emphasised that in joint name cases for it to be found that the actual intention is that the property is to be held other than 50:50 (i.e. to displace the presumption of beneficial joint tenancy) there needs to be an express intention or an inferred intention based on conduct. When it comes to quantification of that interest then it is permissible to impute intention. See Hayward (2016) for a comment on this case.

What if the property is bought as a commercial investment? In *Marr* v *Collie* (2017) it was held that the principles in *Stack* v *Dowden* should not be confined to domestic situations. The parties' common intention, or lack of it, was the key to determining whether the beneficial ownership should reflect the joint legal ownership, or if a resulting trust might be the appropriate solution.

Impress your examiner

A vital point in cases of joint ownership is exactly how the beneficial interests are recorded on the transfer – Form TR1. Research this area and note that the Land Registry does not propose to implement the recommendations for change made by an expert working party which it convened in response to *Stack* v *Dowden*.

Impress your examiner

Refer to the article by Gardner and Davidson (2012) where the question of how to establish common intention in these types of cases is linked to the context of the parties' relationship: 'For the common intention in this context has a significance quite different from a settlor's wish to create an express trust. It is not so much an act of autonomous will, whether by one party or two. It is rather, in its quality as an *agreement*, an instantiation of the trusting and collaborative, and so naturally informal, essence of the parties' familial relationship.' They also point out that although the law respects genuine intentions, out of a libertarian respect for autonomy, the reason for respecting intentions in this context is more a communitarian one, focused on supporting the implications of the family relationship.

Don't be tempted to . . .

Don't fail to understand the debate about exactly how the 'common intention' of the parties is to be ascertained. Note Lady Hale's words: 'the parties' shared intentions, actual, inferred or imputed'. Does the word 'imputed' allow the courts to decide what the parties' intentions were? Note that Lady Hale also emphasised that it is not for the court to impose 'its own view of what is fair on the situation'. But is that precisely what her approach allows the courts to do? Note the views of Lord Wilson in *Jones* v *Kernott*. Finding a common intention is often artificial as the reality is that people do not usually discuss these matters when property is acquired as they do not anticipate their relationship coming to an end. This is also relevant to 'Situation two', discussed next.

Situation two: sole name cases – the property is held in the name of one person and the claim is by another person who claims a beneficial interest

Don't be tempted to . . .

Confuse the position where it is a sole name case with where it is a joint name case. See Gardner (2015) Heresy or not? – in family property. 4 *Conv.* 332 who argues that this is exactly what happened in *Bhura* v *Bhura* (2014).

Common intention

The extent to which a common intention is required has ebbed and flowed over the years. The leading case on this is still *Rosset* (see following box) but *Stack* v *Dowden* and *Jones* v *Kernott* represented a wider view of how common intention is to be established than does *Rosset*. With the latest case, *Capehorn* v *Harris*, we seem to have gone back to *Rosset* principles and this is now the case to apply when you have a sole name case in a problem question in an exam.

Lloyds Bank v *Rosset* [1991] 1 AC 107 (HL)

Facts
It is the legal principle that is vital here: not the facts, although they are interesting.

Legal principle
Lord Bridge held that common intention can be established by:

(a) express discussions that the beneficial interest in the property is to be shared beneficially;

(b) direct contributions to the purchase price by the partner who is not the owner, but he said that it: 'is at least extremely doubtful if anything less will do' thus ruling out indirect contributions of the kind in *Burns* v *Burns* (1984).

Analysis
Part (b) is now almost certainly unduly restrictive in the light of the law today, but *Rosset* is important for the emphasis that it places on common intention, especially in the light of *Capehorn* v *Harris* (discussed next).

Impress your examiner

Look carefully at the facts of this case. Was a different result from that in *Stack* justified?

Capehorn v *Harris* [2015] EWCA Civ 955 (CA)

Facts

The property was in the name of Mrs Capehorn (C) and the claim to a beneficial interest in the property was by her partner, Mr Harris (H) with whom she had cohabited for many years. C had paid the deposit and also funded the mortgage repayments. After H was declared bankrupt his business was continued by C as a sole trader but H had the main business contacts and was the dominant force in running it.

Legal principle

Slade LJ, with whom the other judges agreed, applied a two-stage analysis dealing with the acquisition and then the quantification issue. He held that in deciding if a beneficial interest existed at all (the acquisition issue): 'the person claiming the beneficial interest must show that there was an agreement that he should have a beneficial interest in the property owned by his partner'. If this was so then at the quantification stage, if there is no agreement as to the extent of the interest, 'the court may impute an intention that the person was to have a fair beneficial share in the asset and may assess the quantum of the fair share in the light of all the circumstances'.

Analysis

This case represents a very welcome clarification of the law. The judgment is notably concise on the law and avoids detailed analysis of earlier authorities. Slade LJ is clear that when he refers to an agreement this does not only mean an express agreement, but also cases where one can 'be inferred from conduct in an appropriate case'. Thus of the three types of intention, express or inferred intention is needed to establish a beneficial interest but, in addition to these, imputed intention will also suffice to establish the extent of the interest.

Note two types of claims, both of which often appear in exam questions.

Example 4.1(a)

John and his partner, Joan, live at Pine Lodge. The house is in John's name but Joan contributed 10 per cent of the deposit when John bought it and her earnings as a solicitor pay the household bills enabling John's income as a plumber to be used to pay off the mortgage. They have no children.

Joan claims a share in the property.

Example 4.1(b)

Fred and his partner, Molly, live at Stone Cottage. The house was bought by Molly in 1990 and Fred moved in with her in 1993. They have five children. Molly is an interior designer and she and Fred decided that, in view of her greater earning power, she should continue to work and Fred would stay at home and look after their five children. Thus, Molly's earnings both pay off the mortgage and all other bills.

Fred claims a share in the property.

These are both sole name cases and the first issue will be whether Joan, in Example 4.1(a), and Fred, in Example 4.1(b), can establish if they have a beneficial interest based either on express agreement, or if it can be inferred from conduct. This is established by *Capehorn* v *Harris*. There is no actual evidence of an express agreement but it will be easier to infer one in Example 4.1(a) where there is a direct contribution to the cost of acquisition than in Example 4.1(b) where there is not. Even so, in Example 4.1(b) there seems no reason in principle why the courts cannot infer an agreement and Lady Hale's list of factors in *Stack* v *Dowden* (earlier) could be used here.

Exam tip

In problem questions on sole name cases start with the *Lloyds Bank* v *Rosset* approach and then go on to *Capehorn* v *Harris* which develops the *Rosset* approach. In essay questions you may need to consider earlier cases, for example *Eves* v *Eves* (1975) and *Burns* v *Burns*, to trace the development of the law and demonstrate differing judicial approaches.

Jones v Kernott [2011] UKSC 53 (SC)

Facts

These were given earlier but do not relate to this point.

Legal principle

The Supreme Court followed *Stack* v *Dowden* and held that where a family home was put into the name of one party only, the first issue was whether it was intended that the other party should have any beneficial interest at all: there was no presumption of joint beneficial ownership, but their common intention had again to be deduced from their conduct.

Note Lord Kerr who recognised what imputing an intention really means: 'in the final analysis, the exercise is wholly unrelated to ascertainment of the parties' views. It involves the court deciding what is fair in the light of the whole course of dealing with the property.'

Analysis

This case is included again to emphasise that we are now concerned with the principles applicable to purchases in one name only. In essence this decision merely develops the law but note the remarks of Lord Kerr which go further than some other judges.

Impress your examiner

Point out that although one would think from *Stack* v *Dowden* and *Jones* v *Kernott* that this area of the law is moving in a clear direction, we cannot be sure and some courts still apply *Rosset*. Also look at *Chaudhary* v *Chaudhary* (2013) where in a dispute between stepmother and stepson straightforward resulting trust principles were applied.

Quantification of the beneficial interest

Exam tip

Make sure that you deal with this completely separately from the preceding question of whether a party has a beneficial interest at all. Do not confuse the two!

The leading authority is *Oxley* v *Hiscock* (2004), where Chadwick LJ said that: 'each is entitled to that share which the court considers fair having regard to the whole course of dealing between them in relation to the property'. And in that context, 'the whole course of dealing between them in relation to the property' includes the arrangements they make from time to time in order to meet the outgoings (e.g. mortgage contributions, council tax and utilities, repairs, insurance and housekeeping) which have to be met if they are to live in the property as their home. This reasoning was applied in *Stack* v *Dowden*, *Jones* v *Kernott* and *Capehorn* v *Harris*.

Note that the use by Chadwick LJ of the word 'fair' shows that this approach is a broad one and is based, to some extent, on judicial discretion. Also, although the decision predates *Stack* v *Dowden*, it was approved in that case and in *Fowler* v *Barron* (2008).

Impress your examiner

There is still no authoritative guidance from the courts on what constitutes a fair share of the property. The problems which this can cause are illustrated in *Graham-York* v *York* (2015). One useful point was made by Tomlinson LJ: 'in deciding in such a case what shares are fair, the court is not concerned with some form of redistributive justice. Thus it is irrelevant that it may be thought a "fair" outcome for a woman who has endured years of abusive conduct by her partner to be allotted a substantial interest in his property on his death'. (This had apparently been the case in this instance). See Gardner (2016).

Giving effect to the beneficial interest of a party

In a problem question you should point out that, as this is equity, the beneficial interest will be held on a tenancy in common unless there is an intention to hold as joint tenants, as seemed to be the case in *Stack* v *Dowden*. See *Bull* v *Bull* (1955).

Where is the law in England and Wales going?

The Law Commission in its Report 307 (2007), 'Cohabitation: the financial consequences of relationship breakdown', proposed a scheme where parties to a relationship could claim on the basis of:

- **economic advantage** (the retention of some economic benefit arising from contributions made by the other party during the relationship); or
- **economic disadvantage** (economic sacrifices made as result of that party's contribution to the relationship or resulting from continuing childcare responsibilities following separation).

The effect would have been to widen the net for possible claimants. Look at *Burns* v *Burns* and see if the claimant would have succeeded under these proposals. A number of Private Members' Bills, of which the latest was the Cohabitation Rights Bill 2017, which would give effect to these proposals, have been introduced into the House of Lords but are unlikely to become law.

In February 2018 the Government agreed to review the position again but at the time of writing there is no further news.

Impress your examiner

You will boost your marks by knowledge of the position in other jurisdictions. In brief, the courts adopt wider approaches than has been the case in England, at least until *Stack v Dowden*. See, for example:

- *Soulos* v *Korkontzilas* (1997) – Canada: remedial constructive trust and unjust enrichment. Note in particular the decisions of the Canadian Supreme Court in *Kerr* v *Baranow* (2011) and *Vanasse* v *Seguin* (2011) which utilised the principles of unjust enrichment as applied in Canada.

- *Gilles* v *Keogh* (1989) – New Zealand: meeting the reasonable expectations of the parties but is it now?

- *Baumgartner* v *Baumgartner* (1987) and *Muchinski* v *Dodds* (1981) – Australia: unconscionability.

Putting it all together

Sample question

Could you answer this question? Below is a typical problem question that could arise on this topic. Additionally, a sample essay question and guidance on tackling it can be found on the companion website.

Problem question

Robert and Josephine met in 2013 and decided to set up home together. They bought The Laurels, a registered freehold property, for £300,000 with the aid of a mortgage of £100,000 from the Friendly Building Society secured by a legal charge over the property. Josephine was registered as sole proprietor as Robert's earnings as a proofreader fluctuated greatly. Robert contributed 5 per cent of the deposit from his savings but Josephine paid the rest and she initially assumed responsibility for the mortgage repayments.

In 2015 Robert said to Josephine: 'I realise what a financial drain these payments must be to you. From now on, I will pay all the utility bills so that your earnings are used for the mortgage repayments.' Josephine replied: 'It's about time that you contributed to our joint venture.' Robert, feeling guilty after Josephine's words, then started to begin work on an extension to the house to give them extra room when their family arrived.

In 2019 Josephine needed money to expand a business venture of hers and so, while Robert was on a six-month expedition to Tibet, she took out a loan from the Newtown Bank, secured by a second legal charge on The Laurels.

Josephine's business has failed and she cannot meet the repayments on either mortgage.

Advise Robert what rights, if any, he has in respect of The Laurels.

Would it make any difference to your answer if title to The Laurels was unregistered?

Note: You should be aware that this problem question is probably longer than you might find in the exam as a section has been included asking you the position if title to the house was unregistered. This is to make sure that you recall the difference between registered and unregistered land!

Answer guidelines

Approaching the question

This question involves two areas and you must spend time on each in order to gain a good pass. Do not rush into the issue of whether Robert's beneficial interest binds the mortgagees before you decide if he does, in fact, have a beneficial interest.

Does Robert have a beneficial interest? Consider the following:

- The parties are not married – nor is there any express declaration of trust to satisfy section 53(1)(b), LPA 1925 – so Robert's claim is under the sole name rules.

- This is 'Situation two' (earlier) and the likely claim is under a constructive trust – is there a common intention regarding the beneficial interests? Note that Josephine referred to 'our joint venture' some time after acquisition. Does this make a difference?

Important points to include

- Consider acquisition of the beneficial interest first: *Lloyds Bank* v *Rosset* and then go on to *Capehorn* v *Harris*.

- Emphasise that this is a sole name case unlike the joint name cases of *Stack* v *Dowden* and *Jones* v *Kernott*.

- It is likely that Robert will succeed.

- Then consider:

  (a) quantification of the beneficial interest – *Oxley* v *Hiscock*;

  (b) Robert may be a tenant in common in equity of The Laurels and entitled to share in the proceeds of a sale.

Then consider whether Robert's rights are binding on:

(a) The first mortgagee – Friendly Building Society. No, he gets no interest in the property until completion – *Abbey National* v *Cann* and *Paddington BS* v *Mendelsohn* (see Chapter 2).

(b) The second mortgagee – Newtown Bank. This is a post-acquisition mortgage so Robert's interest may be binding if it overrides that of the bank. Apply Schedule 3, Paragraph 2, LRA 2002 and note that Robert's absence may not deprive him of his interest – see cases on what constitutes actual occupation (see Chapter 2).

If Robert's interest does bind the bank, Robert does have a right to occupy under section 12 of TLATA, but the bank could still apply for a sale – apply section 14 of TLATA and the criteria in section 15 together with *Bank of Baroda* v *Dhillon* (see Chapter 3).

If title was unregistered, then answer (a) would be the same but, as far as the Newtown Bank is concerned, Robert's equitable interest would be binding on it if it had notice. (See *Kingsnorth Finance Co.* v *Tizard*, where interests under trusts are not registrable as land charges – see Chapters 1 and 2.)

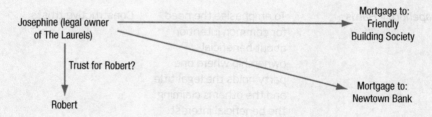

Josephine (legal owner of The Laurels) → Mortgage to: Friendly Building Society

Trust for Robert? → Robert

Josephine → Mortgage to: Newtown Bank

Impress your examiner

Mention one or more of the following in your answer:

- Case law post-*Stack* v *Dowden*.
- Lord Neuberger's divergent view in *Stack* v *Dowden*.
- The views of Lords Kerr and Wilson in *Jones* v *Kernott*.
- Look at *Begum* v *Issa* (2014) – see Chapter 3.
- Law Commission's proposals.

Key case summary

Key case	How to use	Related topics
Stack v *Dowden*	To explain how the courts approach deciding questions of beneficial entitlement to the family home where the legal title is held as joint tenants.	Constructive trusts.

▶

Key case	How to use	Related topics
Jones v *Kernott*	To show the application and development of the principles in *Stack* v *Dowden*.	Constructive trusts.
Lloyds Bank v *Rosset*	To explain the common intention test which was the main authority before *Stack* v *Dowden* and is still used today.	Constructive trusts.
Capehorn v *Harris*	To emphasise the need for common intention about beneficial ownership where one party holds the legal title and the other is claiming the beneficial interest.	Constructive trusts.

Key further reading

Key articles/reports	How to use	Related topics
Gardner, S. (2016) The ongoing evolution of family property constructive trusts. 132 *LQR* 373.	This article looks in detail at *Graham-York* v *York* and is critical of the failure by the courts to develop any clear principles to decide what is meant by 'fairness' in deciding the extent of beneficial shares in trusts of the family home.	Trusts of the family home. Constructive trusts.
Gardner, S. and Davidson, K. (2012) The Supreme Court on family homes. 128 *LQR* 178–83.	This article looks at how establishing a common intention in these types of cases is linked to the context of the parties' relationship. It suggests that one approach to evaluating different ways of deciding how beneficial interests in the family home should be decided is to look at the question from the standpoint of autonomy versus communitarianism.	Trusts of the family home.

Key articles/reports	How to use	Related topics
Hayward, A. (2013) Stack v Dowden (2007); Jones v Kernott (2011). Finding a home for 'family property'. In Gravells N. (ed.) *Landmark Cases in Land Law*, Oxford: Hart Publishing.	This gives a really valuable context for these two vital cases with some interesting factual detail and valuable conclusions.	Trusts of the family home.
Hayward, A. (2016) Case comment on *Barnes v Phillips*. 3 *Conv.* 333.	This is valuable in highlighting a post-*Stack* v *Dowden* and *Jones* v *Kernott* decision and showing how the principles in these cases are being applied by the courts.	Trusts of the family home.
Law Commission (2007) Report 307, *Cohabitation: the financial consequences of relationship breakdown.*	Although this report has not been acted on its proposals are still discussed and are essential for essay questions in this area.	Essays on trusts of the home.

go.pearson.com/uk/lawexpress

Go online to access more revision support including quizzes to test your knowledge, sample questions with answer guidelines, printable versions of the topic maps, and more!

5

Licences. Proprietary estoppel

Revision checklist

Essential points you should know:

- Distinction between licences and property rights
- Types of licences
- Do contractual licences create interests in land?
- Conditions for proprietary estoppel to apply and distinction between proprietary and promissory estoppel
- Recent case law on proprietary estoppel

Topic map

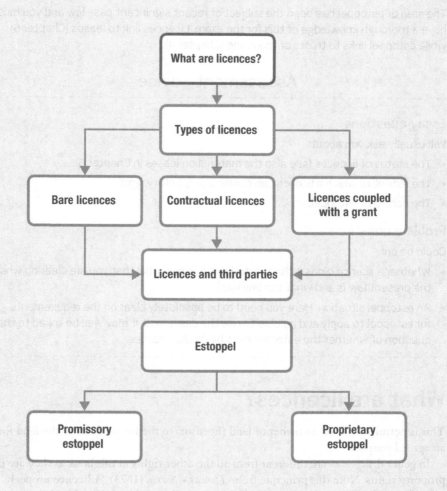

What are licences?

↓

Types of licences

Bare licences   **Contractual licences**   **Licences coupled with a grant**

Licences and third parties

Estoppel

Promissory estoppel   **Proprietary estoppel**

Introduction

This chapter deals with two areas, which may be linked in a question on estoppel licences or may be the subject of two different questions – one on licences and one on proprietary estoppel.

The area of estoppel has been the subject of recent significant case law and you must have a thorough knowledge of this for the exam. Licences link to leases (Chapter 6) while estoppel links to trusts of the home (Chapter 4).

Assessment advice

Essay questions

Will usually ask you about:

- The status of licences (see also the material on leases in Chapter 6).
- The extent to which a licence can confer a proprietary right.
- The nature of estoppel.

Problem questions

Could be on:

- *Whether a licence binds a third party.* Here it is essential that you are clear on what the present law *is* and what the law *was*!
- *An estoppel situation.* Here you need to be absolutely clear on the requirements for estoppel to apply and be able to use the cases well. It may well be linked to the question of whether the estoppel right binds third parties.

What are licences?

This is permission from an owner of land (licensor) to the licensee to use the land for an agreed purpose.

In general, **licences** are different from all the other rights in this book as they are not property rights. Note this principle from *Thomas* v *Sorrell* (1673): 'A licence properly passeth no interest nor alters or transfers property in any thing' (Vaughan CJ).

There are various types of licences:

Bare licences

Licences given without any consideration from the licensee, i.e. when you are invited to someone's house for a party. They can be withdrawn by the licensor at any time.

Licences coupled with a grant

Where the licence is linked to an interest in the land, e.g. a licence to go on to land to collect wood. The right to collect wood is a profit.

Impress your examiner

In *Hurst* v *Picture Theatres Ltd* (1915) the court held that a cinema ticket could grant an interest in land but this was criticised by Latham CJ in the Australian case of *Cowell* v *Rosehill Racecourse* (1937), where he pointed out that the decision in *Hurst* 'ignores the distinction between a personal and a property right'. *Hurst* was really a contractual licence.

It is misleading even to talk of licences here, as the right to go on to the land is really part of the profit. These licences will last as long as the right to which they are attached.

Contractual licences

Where a licence is given for valuable consideration.

Don't be tempted to . . .

Make sure that you are clear on when licences can be revoked. At common law contractual licences and bare licences can in principle be revoked at any time, although equitable remedies may be used to restrain a breach. There is no problem with bare licences, but where a person has paid for a licence, it has seemed unfair for it to be capable of being revoked and this has led to a good deal of case law, beginning with *Wood* v *Leadbitter* (1845), a case which makes a good starting point for essay questions.

Example 5.1

I pay £100 for a ticket to a test match. I am just starting to enjoy the game when an attendant tells me to leave. I am just told to go with no reason and, when I refuse, I am forcibly ejected. It seems that I had been mistaken for someone else who was a troublemaker.

Winter Garden Theatre (London) Ltd v Millennium Productions Ltd [1947] 2 All ER 331 (HL)

Facts
The owners of a theatre licensed it for six months to Millennium Productions but later gave them one month's notice to leave, after Millennium Productions had contracted with a production company for it to put on a play at the theatre for six months.

Legal principle
A licence can be revoked on giving reasonable notice, and here the revocation was valid.

Analysis
When equitable remedies became available in all courts after the Judicature Acts 1873–5, injunctions and specific performance in particular became available to protect a licensee. In this case the HL said, *obiter*, that where a contractual licence is, on its terms, irrevocable, then revocation in breach of contract can be restrained by injunction. Note especially *Verrall* v *Great Yarmouth Borough Council* (1980) as an example of the use of an equitable remedy to enforce a licence.

Exam tip

The topic of revocability of licences is a favourite one in essays and you should read the different cases carefully. Make sure that you stress this one simple point: could a licence be revoked (cancelled) at any time or should it be treated as an interest in land, like other land law rights? If it can be revoked, is notice required?

Licences are also important in connection with leases as a licensee of property has no security of tenure. (Check Chapter 6 to make sure that you understand this.) You could bring this point into your essay on licences.

Impress your examiner

Lateral thinking across different subjects always gains marks where relevant. Here is a thought: is there a tort of violating the enjoyment of a contractual licence? If third parties are under a duty not to do so then contractual licensees have a corresponding (non-proprietary) right against them. See Baker (2019).

Licences and third parties

In an answer start by distinguishing between:

- **bare licences** – cannot bind third parties;
- **licences coupled with a grant** – if the grant confers a proprietary interest in land then the licence, as linked to the grant, will bind third parties;
- **contractual licences** – this is the problem area.

Exam tip

- -

Licences and third parties are a favourite topic for essay questions.

- -

The following case lays down the orthodox view.

King v *David Allen Ltd* [1916] 2 AC 54 (HL)

Facts
A licence was granted allowing the fixing of advertisements to the wall of a cinema. The licensor then granted a lease of the cinema to a third party.

Legal principle
The grant of the lease had ended the contractual licence.

Analysis
This establishes that as a licence is not an interest in land it cannot bind successors in title. This is the fundamental, orthodox view.

Note attempts by the courts to make contractual licences binding on third parties:

- *Errington* v *Errington and Woods* (1952): a contractual licence can bind third parties.
- *Binions* v *Evans* (1972): use of a constructive trust to hold that a licence can bind a purchaser.
- *Ashburn Anstalt* v *Arnold* (1988): attempts to make contractual licences binding on third parties were disapproved. See the judgment of Fox LJ.

Proprietary estoppel

The essential elements of proprietary estoppel are:

- a commitment or promise by one person (X) to another (Y);
- which X intends Y to rely on;

- and where Y's actual reliance to his detriment is reasonable in the circumstances;
- an objective test applies: thus the question is whether a promise by X can reasonably be understood as a commitment by X to Y.

The basis of the doctrine can be seen as unconscionability: would it be unconscionable for X, when Y has relied on X's promise to his detriment, to then depart from that promise?

Exam tip

Note that estoppel is an example of equity: this means that there is a good deal of discretion in this area and it is unwise to come to a black-and-white conclusion.

Example 5.2

X owns a piece of land and says to Y: 'You can have it as a market garden.' Y takes over the land and develops it as a market garden but the land is never conveyed to him. X later attempts to turn Y out.

Here there is no deed of conveyance but equity provides that it could be unjust to allow a person in X's position to rely on this fact, so it may be remedied by the doctrine of proprietary estoppel.

Proprietary estoppel and promissory estoppel

Promissory estoppel applies in contractual relationships and essentially operates as a defence to prevent a party from going back on a promise.

Proprietary estoppel applies in property as well as contractual situations and can give rights where none existed before.

Impress your examiner

Consider the link between proprietary estoppel and common intention constructive trusts (see *Lloyds Bank plc* v *Rosset* (1991) in Chapter 4 and *Herbert* v *Doyle* (2010) later). However, a commonly held view is that they are different: in *Stack* v *Dowden* (2007) Lord Walker said: 'Proprietary estoppel typically consists of asserting an equitable claim against the conscience of the "true" owner. . . . It is to be satisfied by the minimum award necessary to do justice . . . which may sometimes lead to no more than a monetary award. A "common intention" constructive trust, by contrast, is identifying the true beneficial owner or owners, and the size of their beneficial interests.'

In *Crossco No. 4 Unlimited and others* v *Jolan* (2011) it was claimed that the defendants could not terminate a commercial lease because of estoppel and a constructive trust. The claim failed, but this is yet another illustration of the relationship between the two concepts.

Examples of proprietary estoppel

- *Inwards* v *Baker* (1965): a father allowed his son to build a bungalow on land owned by the father. The son was granted a licence for life.
- *Gillett* v *Holt* (2000): even though a promise to leave property to X by will is superseded by a will which leaves the same property to Y, estoppel can still apply.

Estoppel: recent developments

The nature of proprietary estoppel has been the subject of important cases which you must be fully aware of for your exam.

Yeoman's Row Management Ltd v *Cobbe* [2008] UKHL 55

Facts
An oral agreement between the company and Cobbe provided that a block of flats owned by the company would be demolished and Cobbe would apply for planning permission to erect houses in their place, with any excess of the proceeds over £24 million shared equally with the company. After planning permission had been obtained, the company went back on the oral agreement and demanded more money. Cobbe claimed that the company was estopped from going back on the agreement.

Legal principle
Estoppel did not apply. No specific property right had been promised to Cobbe nor would it be unconscionable for the company to go back on its assurance. The parties had intentionally not entered into any legally binding arrangement while Mr Cobbe sought to obtain planning permission and had left matters on a speculative basis, each knowing full well that neither was legally bound.

Analysis
Lord Scott held that proprietary estoppel requires clarity as to 'what the object of the estoppel in question is to be estopped from denying'. He also made other remarks which are considered later.

Thorner v *Major* [2009] UKHL 18

Facts

D had worked at P's farm for no payment from 1976 onwards and, by the 1980s, hoped that he might inherit the farm. No express representation had ever been made, but D relied on various hints and remarks made by P over the years. Also in 1990, P gave D a bonus notice relating to two policies on P's life, saying 'that's for my death duties'.

Legal principle

The handing over of the bonus notice in 1990 should not be considered alone, and the evidence had demonstrated a continuing pattern of conduct by P for the remaining 15 years of his life, which was sufficient to amount to an estoppel.

Analysis

The case also illustrated the possibility of relying on 'oblique assurances' in family inheritance cases whereas in *Cobbe* Lord Scott held that 'clarity' was needed. Lord Scott's approach was felt to be appropriate in commercial contexts. See also *James* v *James* later.

Don't be tempted to . . .

Be careful that you discuss the underlying debate and do not just give the facts of these two cases. Start with McFarlane (2009).

James v *James* [2018] EWHC 43 (Ch)

Facts

The deceased had built up a substantial business and the claimant had worked for it for several years, living rent-free in a property belonging to the deceased. The deceased made a will in 2010, leaving his remaining land and farming business to his family but nothing to the claimant who maintained that he had acted to his detriment in relying upon an assurance from the deceased that another parcel of land in the farming business would become his.

Legal principle

The court held that the claimant 'could not produce any particular promise or act creating an expectation, intended to be relied upon, that the testator would leave any particular property to him, let alone the whole of it' and so his claim failed.

Analysis

This decision is criticised by Carroll (2018) in that there was no consideration of the culmination of assertions made consistently to the son from infancy, well into adulthood, 'that he stood to farm those parcels of land in the place of his father one day'. On this basis this decision contrasts with *Thorner* v *Major* where a much broader view of what is needed to constitute representations was taken.

Herbert v *Doyle* [2010] EWCA Civ 1095

Facts

Owners of two adjoining properties, X and Y, had verbally agreed on transfers of parking spaces on their land, provided that a number of conditions were satisfied.

Legal principle

The agreement did not satisfy section 2(1) of the Law of Property (Miscellaneous) Provisions Act 1989 (see Chapter 1). However, the parties had come to a sufficiently certain agreement, made orally, which created a constructive trust over their respective parts of the property.

Analysis

Although the actual decision was that there was a constructive trust, the language used by the CA was that of proprietary estoppel. This is because section 2(5) of the Law of Property (Miscellaneous) Provisions Act 1989 provides that it does not affect the operation of resulting, implied or constructive trusts (i.e. no writing needed) but does not mention estoppel. See Owen and Rees (2011).

Impress your examiner

Take the point just made further and explain that in *Whitaker* v *Kinnear* (2011) the court held that proprietary estoppel in a case involving the sale of land *had* survived the enactment of section 2 of the Law of Property (Miscellaneous) Provisions Act 1989. Note also *Matchmove Ltd* v *Dowding* (2016) which concerned one party resiling from an oral agreement for the sale of land. This was regarded by the CA as a common intention constructive trust case and so within section 2(5).

Exam tip

In an answer on estoppel consider if the claim could be linked with one based on a common intention constructive trust.

The debate in *Yeomans Row* v *Cobbe* and *Thorner* v *Major*

Lord Scott in *Yeomans Row* v *Cobbe* considered that proprietary estoppel should be restricted to representations of specific facts, or mixed law and fact by X, which stood in the way of a right claimed by Y. However, this seemed to mean that proprietary estoppel was no different to promissory estoppel: it only applied as a defence to an action where those specific representations had been gone back on, and not to enable an independent right to be asserted. Moreover, this approach would have meant that proprietary estoppel could not have applied in cases involving a promise of an inheritance as this would relate to a *future* right, as in *Thorner* v *Major* itself.

Lord Scott would have upheld the claim in *Thorner* v *Major* on the basis of a remedial constructive trust instead, as when the promise was made there was no specific property to which it could apply. The other judges, however, applied proprietary estoppel. See the 'Key further reading' section at the end of this chapter for references to a discussion of this debate and the companion Law Express book, *Equity and Trusts*, for details of the remedial constructive trust.

See also *Macdonald* v *Frost* (2009), where the lack of any assurance was fatal to the claim.

Impress your examiner

Point out, especially in an essay question, that the Law Commission (2008) (Consultation Paper 186) considered whether proprietary estoppel could replace prescription as a method of acquisition of an easement (see Chapter 8) but did not favour the idea. (See Paras 4.187–4.192.) This is a useful link with another area.

Once estoppel has been established the court must decide the remedy.

Jennings v Rice [2003] EWCA Civ 159 (CA)

Facts

X worked for nearly 30 years as a gardener and odd-job man for Y. He was initially paid but then Y promised him that she would leave him her house and that he would be 'all right one day'. After this he was no longer paid. Y died intestate. X claimed either Y's whole estate (value: £1,285,000) or the value of the house (£435,000).

Legal principle

X would be awarded £200,000 as a larger sum would have been out of all proportion to what X might have charged for his services.

Analysis

In a claim based on proprietary estoppel the court has a discretion as to what remedy to award in order to 'feed the estoppel' and as Lord Walker said in *Stack* v *Dowden* (2007) is 'satisfied by the minimum award necessary to do justice'. This may lead to the promisee receiving less than he had expected.

Don't be tempted to . . .

Don't omit a discussion of how the estoppel will be satisfied. Remember that this is equity and so the court has discretion. The basic point is that any equitable right is inchoate until it crystallises in the form of an order made by the court, which gives the claimant a specific interest.

In the important decision in *Davies* v *Davies* [2016], the CA held that proportionality is at the heart of the doctrine of proprietary estoppel and so there must be proportionality 'between remedy and detriment' to 'avoid an unconscionable result, and a disproportionate remedy'. Although there may be cases where the expectation of the claimant would be an appropriate place to begin, where this expectation is disproportionate to the detriment the court should satisfy the equity in a more limited way.

Proprietary estoppel and third parties

A right by proprietary estoppel may bind a purchaser where title to the land is registered.

Section 116, Land Registration Act 2002

This provides that, in registered land, an equity by estoppel and a **mere equity** have effect from the moment they arise as an interest capable of binding successors in title. Therefore, it can be protected by a notice against the title.

In addition, if the person claiming the estoppel is in occupation, under it he or she may have an overriding interest under Schedule 3, Paragraph 2, LRA 2002.

Note *Scott v Southern Pacific Mortgages* (2014) where it was confirmed by the Supreme Court that section 116 of the LRA did not apply where a person only had a personal interest in property.

Mere equity

A mere equity arises where there is a right in equity to apply for a remedy, such as specific performance of a contract for the sale of land. Questions involving section 116 of the LRA are much more likely to involve an equity by estoppel.

Example 5.3

- -

X claims to be entitled to Blackacre as Y, the freehold owner, had told him that he could have the land and X had erected a building on it. Y then sells the land to Z. X will then claim against Y that Y is estopped from denying X's title to the land. If the court grants the order, X will have an equitable interest which, under section 116, is taken to have arisen at the time when the facts giving rise to the estoppel took place. Thus:

- there was an estoppel at the time of the disposition by Y to Z;
- this is an equitable interest in the land;
- assuming X was in occupation under this interest at the time of the disposition by Y to Z (see Sch. 3 Para. 2, LRA 2002);
- X can have an overriding interest which binds Z.

This is a really excellent way to round off an answer to a problem question on estoppel!

Putting it all together

Sample question

Could you answer this question? Below is a typical problem question that could arise on this topic. Additionally, a sample essay question and guidance on tackling it can be found on the companion website.

Problem question

Emily is the daughter of Claire, who has recently died. When Claire was aged 50, Emily gave up her job as a solicitor to move in and look after her mother, and she continued to do this until Claire died, aged 82. Claire was disabled and there had been an informal arrangement that Claire's Employment and Support Allowance would be paid to Emily to meet the needs of them both. In addition, Emily drew a carer's allowance for looking after her mother. Utility and other bills were paid out of Claire's savings.

Claire often said to Emily: 'I don't know what I would do without you. When I am gone you will have a secure home.' Emily assumed that Claire meant that she would leave her the house.

Claire has died intestate and has left seven children, including Emily, and under the intestacy rules the house will go to them equally.

Advise Emily on whether she has any rights in the house which are binding on the other children.

Would your answer differ if all the other children had signed a document 10 years ago stating that, when Claire died, they would allow Emily to remain at the house?

Answer guidelines

Approaching the question

This question requires a thorough knowledge of the conditions for an estoppel to apply and, for a good mark, an in-depth knowledge of the case law and recognition that, as this is equity, there are no black-and-white answers!

Important points to include

- Apply conditions for an estoppel.
- Representation – what Claire said? Note *Thorner* v *Major* and then *James* v *James*.
- Relied on by Emily? Emily assumed that Claire meant that she would leave her the house.
- To Emily's detriment? Note that Emily drew a carer's allowance.

Cases – you must demonstrate a clear grasp of *Yeomans Row* v *Cobbe* and *Thorner* v *Major*. *Gillett* v *Holt* is also relevant.

Consider unconscionability:

- If Emily succeeds, what will the remedy be?
- The court has discretion. Apply *Jennings* v *Rice*.
- Document signed by the children – does it mean that Emily's rights bind them?
- Look, e.g. at *Binions* v *Evans*, but *Ashburn Anstalt* v *Arnold* emphasises that *Binions* is no longer an authority for the proposition that contractual licences can bind third parties.
- Her right could be registered. Apply section 116, LRA 2002.

Impress your examiner

- Discussion of Lord Scott's analysis in *Thorner* v *Major* – suggestion that a remedial constructive trust would be more appropriate. Why?
- Compare the extent of detriment in *Suggitt* v *Suggitt* (2012) to that in *Thorner* v *Major* and apply to the question.
- Detailed discussion of the land registration issue angle and Schedule 3, Paragraph 2 LRA 2002.
- Reasoning in cases such as *Ashburn* in detail.

Key case summary

Key case	How to use	Related topics
Winter Garden Theatre (London) Ltd v *Millennium Productions Ltd*	To explain how a licence can be revoked on giving reasonable notice.	Revocation of a licence.
King v *David Allen Ltd*	To demonstrate that as a licence does not create an interest in land it cannot bind third parties.	Licences as merely personal rights.
Yeoman's Row Management Ltd v *Cobbe*	To explain the nature of estoppel and to refer to the view of Lord Scott that estoppel only applies where there is a representation of specific facts/law.	Nature of estoppel.

Key case	How to use	Related topics
Thorner v *Major*	To explain that there can be an estoppel where there is no specific representation but where there is a pattern of conduct.	Conditions for estoppel.
James v *James*	To consider the extent to which clear representations are needed for an estoppel.	Conditions for estoppel.
Herbert v *Doyle*	To explain the application of section 2(1) of the Law of Property (Miscellaneous Provisions) Act 1989.	Estoppel and constructive trusts.
Jennings v *Rice*	To show that even though there is an estoppel the promisee may not receive what he/she was promised.	Estoppel as equitable: discretionary.

Key further reading

Key articles/reports	How to use	Related topics
Baker, A. (2019) Violating the enjoyment of a licence: a new tort. 2 *Conv.* 119.	This argues that *Manchester Airport Plc* v *Dutton* is the starting point for a new tort of interfering with a contractual licence.	Contractual licences.
Carroll, E. (2018) 'The assurances are only half the story . . .': proprietary estoppel and testamentary capacity in James v James. 2 *Conv.* 192.	This is useful to read alongside that by Dixon (2019) as it looks especially at the question of the nature of representations needed for a proprietary estoppel.	What is required as evidence of a representation to satisfy an estoppel?
Dixon, M. (2019) Editorial: Proprietary estoppel: the law of farms and families. 2 *Conv.* 82.	This looks at recent cases on estoppel and makes the point that a successful proprietary estoppel does not always lead to the award of a proprietary right.	Nature of estoppel. Remedies.

▶

Key articles/reports	How to use	Related topics
McFarlane, B. (2009) Apocalypse averted: proprietary estoppel in the House of Lords. 125 *LQR* 535.	This is an invaluable analysis and criticism of the controversial decision of the HL in *Cobbe*.	Nature of proprietary estoppel.
Owen, G. and Rees, O. (2011) S. 2(5) of the Law of Property (Miscellaneous) Provisions) Act 1989: a misconceived approach? 6 *Conv.* 495.	This is a valuable article on the problems caused by section 2(5) of the Law of Property (Miscellaneous) Provisions Act 1989 which provides that it does not affect the operation of resulting, implied or constructive trusts but does not mention estoppel. However, this article needs to be read alongside later cases.	Proprietary estoppel and constructive trusts.

go.pearson.com/uk/lawexpress

Go online to access more revision support including quizzes to test your knowledge, sample questions with answer guidelines, printable versions of the topic maps, and more!

6

Leases

Revision checklist

Essential points you should know:

- Distinction between a lease and a licence
- Types of leases
- Legal and equitable leases
- Extent to which leases are binding on a transferee of the land
- Parties to a lease
- When a landlord can refuse consent to an assignment of a lease
- Distinction between express and implied covenants in leases
- Liability where the Landlord and Tenant (Covenants) Act 1995 applies and when it does not
- Remedies for breaches of covenants

Topic map

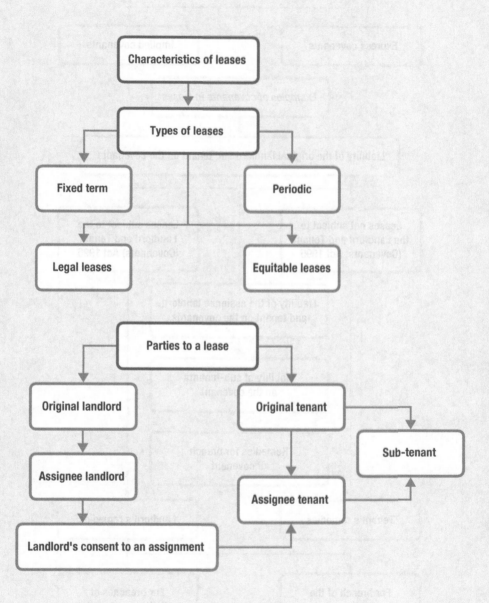

Characteristics of leases

Types of leases

Fixed term

Periodic

Legal leases

Equitable leases

Parties to a lease

Original landlord

Original tenant

Assignee landlord

Sub-tenant

Assignee tenant

Landlord's consent to an assignment

Printable versions of these topic maps are available from **go.pearson.com/uk/lawexpress**

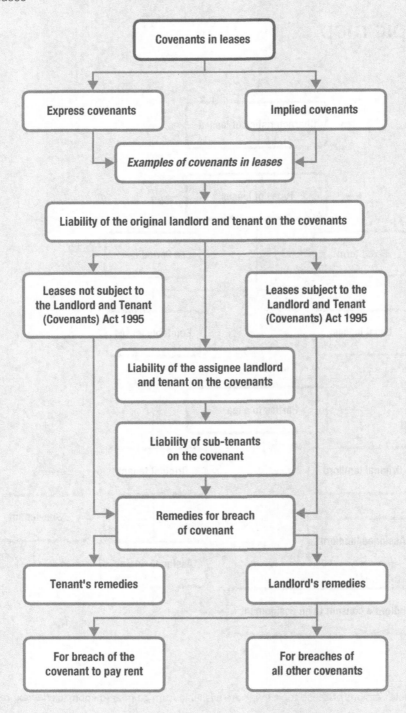

Introduction

There are two distinct areas on which you can expect examination questions: one is the creation of a lease and the distinction between a lease and a licence; the other is covenants in a lease and their enforceability together with remedies.

The difference between a lease and a licence is reasonably straightforward but it is easy to trip up on questions on types of leases: watch out for a periodic tenancy popping up! Questions on covenants contain a number of areas and as always you must adopt a clear logical approach to them.

Assessment advice

Essay questions

A common essay question is to ask you if it matters whether a lease is legal or equitable. The answer is, of course, that it does and you then need to explore this. You could get a more challenging question on the lease/licence distinction or on remedies for breach of covenants.

Problem questions

Examples are:

(a) the lease/licence distinction, possibly linked with what type of lease it is, assuming that it is a lease at all;

(b) whether a lease is binding on a purchaser of the freehold, this could be linked with the question in (a);

(c) whether the lease is binding on a third party;

(d) liability for breach of covenants.

Characteristics of a lease

A lease is an estate in the land which, therefore, gives a proprietary interest in the land.

A **lease** must be distinguished from a licence, which only gives a personal right in the land. Although the fact that licences only create personal interests has proved controversial in the past, it is the law today. Go to Chapters 1 and 5 and revise leases as proprietary interests and licences as personal interests.

Keep in mind two vital consequences of the right being a lease and not a licence:

(1) It can bind third parties, e.g. purchasers of the freehold.

(2) The holder of a lease has security of tenure created by statute but a licensee has not.

The **parties to a lease** are the **landlord** and **tenant**. Note the terminology: whilst the parties to a lease are the landlord and the tenant, they are legally the lessor (landlord) and the lessee (tenant).

Exam tip

You will not be required to know the details of the statutory protection given to tenants in a land law exam unless your syllabus expressly includes landlord and tenant law.

The essential characteristics of a lease

Street v Mountford [1985] 2 All ER 289 (HL)

Facts

Under what was described as a licence agreement, X was given exclusive possession of furnished rooms at a rent. She had signed a statement at the end of the agreement that this was not intended to give rise to a tenancy under the Rent Acts. It was held that in fact she did have a tenancy.

Legal principle

A lease must have three characteristics:

(1) exclusive possession;

(2) for a fixed or periodic term;

(3) at a rent.

If so, there will be a tenancy, unless there are exceptional circumstances which make it a licence.

Analysis

The case shifted the emphasis from whether there is an intention to create a tenancy to whether there is a grant of exclusive possession. Previous case law had used the test of whether there was an intention to create a tenancy. However, this led to landlords trying to evade the Rent Acts by using what were called 'non-occupation residential licence agreements' where in fact there was a tenancy.

The fact that the agreement is described as a licence does not prevent it from being a lease if the above characteristics are present.

Note that there is no absolute principle of no rent, no lease. See *Ashburn Anstalt* v *Arnold* (1988).

There have been many cases which have applied the principles in *Street* v *Mountford*.

Exam tip

The principles in *Street* v *Mountford* are absolutely vital for a problem question on the lease/licence distinction.

Antoniades v *Villiers* [1988] 3 All ER 1058 (HL)

Facts
A couple entered into two separate but identical agreements under which they were given the right to occupy rooms and each had separate responsibility for payment of half the rent. The agreement provided that they were to use the rooms either in common with the owner or with other licensees permitted by him.

Legal principle
Despite the attempt to make this look like two separate licence agreements, it was, in fact, a lease. A vital point was that they had the choice of either two single beds or one double bed. They chose a double bed and so clearly they intended to occupy the rooms jointly.

Analysis
This follows *Street* v *Mountford* in holding that what matters is the intention to have exclusive possession.

Compare this case with *AG Securities* v *Vaughan* (1988).

The lease/licence distinction became less important in the late 1980s after the end of widespread secure tenancies and rent control and the rise of the assured shorthold tenancy. However, it has resurfaced in recent cases examined by Whayman (2019).

Note a common point for exam questions: the landlord retains a set of keys. In *Aslan* v *Murphy* [1990] it was held that this by itself did not prevent a lease.

Exam tip

Do not fall into the trap of saying that exclusive possession will *automatically* create a tenancy. Lord Templeman in *Street* v *Mountford* said that there were circumstances where this would not be so, e.g. where a buyer of a house is allowed into possession before completion of the transfer. Here there is the relationship of buyer and seller, not landlord and tenant. The point is: do the circumstances show that there was no intention to create the relationship of landlord and tenant? Look at, e.g., *Heslop* v *Burns* (1974).

Impress your examiner

In *Bruton* v *London and Quadrant Housing Trust* (1999) the HL indicated that a lease could create purely personal rights between the parties and this 'personal' tenancy is binding on the immediate landlord but not on anyone with a superior title. This decision continues to be the subject of academic debate and criticism. See Baker (2014).

In *London Borough of Islington* v *Green and O'Shea* (2005) the Court of Appeal held that a personal tenancy granted by a person who themselves only has a licence to use property is binding on the licensee who grants it, but not on the licensor (the freeholder) who is not a party to the contractual tenancy.

The rule that a lease must be for a term certain is illustrated by *Prudential Assurance* v *London Residuary Body* (1992): lease granted until a road required for road widening invalid.

Mexfield Housing Co-operative Ltd v *Berrisford* (2011) UKSC 52 (SC)

Facts

The claimant agreed to let a property to the defendant from month to month for a weekly rent. By clause 5, the defendant could only end the agreement by giving one month's notice. By clause 6, the claimant could end the agreement only if, e.g., the rent was in arrears for a certain time.

Legal principle

This was not a monthly periodic tenancy because of clauses 5 and 6 which restricted the circumstances when it could be ended. It would have been void as of uncertain duration but the court held that it took effect as a lease for life and so was saved by the operation of section 149(6) LPA 1925, which converted leases for lives into leases for 90 years.

Analysis

This is a controversial decision and, as we will see in this chapter, its effect has been limited in later cases. The SC did not like the 'term certain' rule but felt unable to abandon it. Instead it avoided its consequences in this case by subtle reasoning.

Impress your examiner

Ask if the requirement that leases must be of certain duration serves any useful purpose. The Law Commission may now investigate this point. Is there a need for a general reform of formalities in property law?

However, the effect of *Mexfield* has been severely limited by *Southward Housing Co-operative* v *Walker* [2015] where it was held that the question was one of intention: did the parties intend to create a lease for life? In *Mexfield* they did; here they did not. Thus the uncertainty of the agreement in this case meant that it could not take effect as a lease; therefore it was a contractual licence and the licensors (i.e. the landlords under the 'lease') obtained possession.

Leases are classified by the length of time they last for and the main types to learn for an exam are:

• lease for a fixed term;
• **periodic tenancy**.

You also need to know two other types of tenancy: **tenancy at will** and **tenancy at sufferance**.

Tenancy at will

The tenant, with the owner's consent, occupies land at the will of the owner, who, therefore, may terminate the tenancy at any time. The tenant has no security of tenure and is really in no better position than a licensee except that as a tenant there is a right to exclusive possession. A tenancy at will can arise where, e.g., a tenant goes into possession pending negotiations for a lease or holds over after the expiry of an existing lease as in *Barclays Wealth Trustees (Jersey) Ltd* v *Erimus Housing Ltd* (2014).

Tenancy at sufferance

The tenant, after the expiry of the lease, continues in possession without the consent of the landlord (remember that a tenant at will does have consent). A tenant at sufferance has no real tenancy and cannot even sue another for trespass (*Schwartz* v *Zamrl* (1968)).

Periodic tenancies

Periodic tenancies often arise in exam questions and it is vital to be able to recognise them: they arise from payment of rent at periodic intervals. There are two types:

(1) *Express periodic tenancies*, e.g. where a tenancy is granted from year to year.

(2) *Implied periodic tenancies*. These are probably more likely in an exam question as they can be linked with a question where the formalities for the creation of an express legal or equitable lease were not observed.

Example 6.1

X agrees by a written agreement to let a flat to Y. The agreement is signed by Y but not by X. However, Y goes into possession and pays rent monthly.

This is not a legal lease by deed nor is it a valid equitable lease as it does not satisfy the requirements of section 2 of the Law of Property (Miscellaneous Provisions) Act 1989 (see later and Chapter 1).

Y may claim a monthly periodic tenancy based on payment of rent. Do point out that there is only a presumption that there is a tenancy – see the CA in *Javad* v *Mohammad Aqil* (1991) but on the facts given in Example 6.1 it is highly likely that one would be implied.

Another example of a periodic tenancy is where there is no agreement at all and the 'tenant' is just allowed into possession and then pays rent at regular intervals. The payment of rent converts what is just a tenancy at will into a periodic tenancy.

Periodic tenancies are likely to be legal (not exceeding three years – see later) and will not require registration (not exceeding seven years – see later). Remember to check the requirements for legal and equitable leases in Chapter 1 and the registration requirements in Chapter 2.

Types of leases

Legal leases

A lease will be legal if created by deed, but there is an important exception: (see below).

Check that you are familiar with what a deed is and the requirements for its creation (see Chapter 1).

Section 54(2), Law of Property Act 1925

A lease not exceeding three years can be legal without any formalities (even oral) if:

- in possession – this means that the tenant must be given an *immediate* right of possession;
- best rent – this probably means the market rent – see *Fitzkriston LLP* v *Panayi* (2008);
- no fine – no premium payable.

Impress your examiner

- -

See Pawlowski (2011): A fresh look at s. 54(2), 15(6) (L & T Review) 216 for an argument that the requirement of a best rent for section 54(2) to apply should be abolished and that the 'in possession' requirement should be replaced by one that the lease should take effect in possession within three months of the grant.

Exam tip

Watch for periodic tenancies (see earlier) in the exam: these will be legal as the length of the lease will be less than three years provided that the requirements of section 54(2) of the LPA are satisfied.

Equitable leases

A lease can be equitable under the principle in *Walsh* v *Lonsdale* (1882) as an agreement for a lease but it must satisfy the three requirements for a valid agreement set out in section 2 of the Law of Property (Miscellaneous Provisions) Act 1989. Check Chapter 1 to make sure that you understand and can apply these requirements.

Walsh v *Lonsdale* [1882] 21 Ch D 9 (HC)

Facts

A lease was granted but not by deed. Thus it was only equitable – an agreement for a lease can be enforced by equity on the basis of the maxim that 'equity looks on that as done which ought to be done', i.e. if a person has agreed to grant a lease then he ought to do so and, as far as possible, equity will assume that he has done so.

Legal principle

An agreement for a lease can create a valid equitable lease.

Analysis

The effect was to allow an equitable defence by the landlord based on his right to specific performance of the agreement enforceable in equity, to a common law claim by the tenant for damages for illegal distress when the landlord claimed rent in advance due under the agreement. However, as agreements are enforceable in equity there is a discretion whether to enforce them: see *Coatsworth* v *Johnson* (1886) where a tenant claimed specific performance of an equitable lease for a farm but this was refused as he was in breach of the covenant to farm with good husbandry.

Don't be tempted to . . .

Don't rush into answering a problem question on types of leases. Take your time and think through a logical approach.

Try this:

- How long is the lease for? If not exceeding three years, it can be legal without formalities, provided that section 54(2), LPA is satisfied.

▶

- If it exceeds three years, was it created by deed? If so, it is legal (and can also be an overriding interest if it does not exceed seven years – see later).
- If there is no deed, then is there an agreement for a lease which satisfies section 2 of the Law of Property (Miscellaneous Provisions) Act 1989? If so, lease will be equitable.
- If tenant pays rent regularly, then can have a periodic tenancy – legal and likely to be overriding as less than seven years.

Comparison between legal and equitable leases

A very common essay question asks you if there are any differences between legal and equitable leases.

Legal leases	Equitable leases
Created by deed except for leases not exceeding three years	Created by agreement which satisfies section 2, Law of Property (Miscellaneous Provisions) Act 1989
Not granted at the discretion of the court	Granted at the discretion of the court – equitable remedies are discretionary
Tenant under a legal lease can claim implied easements under section 62(1), LPA 1925	Tenant under an equitable lease cannot claim implied easements under section 62(1), LPA 1925 – equitable lease is not a conveyance

In addition, there are different rules on whether legal and equitable leases can bind third parties – see under next heading in this chapter.

Check Chapter 8 and make sure that you understand and can apply the rule on creation of easements in section 62(1), LPA 1925.

Leases and third parties

This was dealt with in Chapter 2, and you should check your knowledge of registered land and unregistered land now.

Summary: registered and unregistered land (leases)

Registered land	Unregistered land
Legal leases for over seven years are registrable dispositions	Legal leases are binding on all third parties
Legal leases for less than this period are overriding interests	
Equitable leases should be registered as estate contracts but, if they are not and if the leaseholder is in actual occupation, they may have an overriding interest under Schedule 3, Paragraph 2 of the LRA 2002	Equitable leases need to be protected on the register of land charges as estate contracts: Class C(iv)

Exam tip

When you get a problem question on leases, check the *length* of the leases to see:

- What formalities are needed? – vital length is not exceeding three years.
- If the lease is legal, does it need to be substantively registered? – vital length is not exceeding seven years.

So, think three years and then seven years!

Parties to a lease

The area covered by this chapter often forms a problem question in an exam. The situation can be set out in the following diagram.

Keep this diagram in mind when studying this chapter, and if you get an exam question on this area then make a diagram like this to show who the parties are and their positions.

Note the following terms in Figure 6.1:

- **Lessor**: grantor of the lease.
- **Lessee**: grantee of the lease.
- **Headlease**: lease granted by the lessor to the lessee as distinct from a sub-lease.
- **Freehold reversion**: the rights retained by the lessor on the grant of a lease.

Figure 6.1

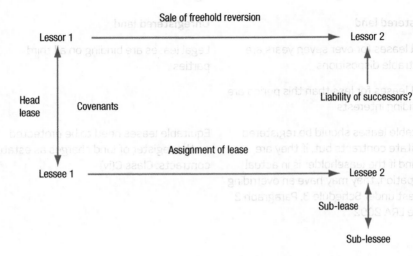

- **Assignment**: disposition of the lessee's interest to the assignee who then takes over the assignor's interest in the land.
- **Underlease/sub-lease**: creation of a subsidiary estate out of the lessee's estate.

Exam tip

When you get a problem question on leases, before you do anything else, you must ask two questions:

(1) Is the lease legal or equitable?

(2) What date was it granted? If it was on or after 1 January 1996, your answer will differ from one if it was before this date as the Landlord and Tenant (Covenants) Act 1995 applies. The actual changes are explained later.

Assignment of leases

Check whether the lease either prohibits an **assignment** altogether or (more likely) allows assignment providing that the landlord consents.

Exam tip

Be prepared for a question asking you to discuss a refusal of consent.

Section 19(1), Landlord and Tenant Act 1927

The landlord must not withhold consent unreasonably.

Consent to an assignment cannot be refused on grounds which have nothing to do with the relationship of landlord and tenant. So, a personal dislike would not be enough.

No.1 West India Quay (Residential) Ltd v East Tower Apartments Ltd [2018] EWCA Civ 250 (CA)

Facts

The landlord refused to grant consent for the assignment of leases because the tenant had refused: (1) to pay the landlord's legal costs; (2) to allow a prior inspection to be carried out by a surveyor, at a cost of £350, to check whether there had been breaches of the underleases; (3) to provide bank references for prospective assignees.

Legal principle

Ground (1) was unreasonable but the other two were reasonable. The reasons were freestanding and so the fact that one was unreasonable did not vitiate the others. The overall decision to withhold consent was reasonable.

Analysis

This is a really important area in practice and this case is interesting as illustrating the reasonableness of different conditions. See also Sissons (2018).

Sections 1(3) and 1(6), Landlord and Tenant Act 1988

Section 1(3): if the tenant asks for consent in writing, the landlord must give or refuse consent in writing and must do this in a reasonable time.
Section 1(6): it is for the landlord to prove that:

- a refusal of consent was reasonable;
- consent was given or withheld in a reasonable time;
- if conditions were imposed, that they were reasonable.

Examples of where a refusal of consent would be reasonable:

- Where the landlord reasonably believes that a proposed assignment would lead to a breach of covenant in the lease – see the HL in *Ashworth Frazer Ltd* v *Gloucester City Council* (2001).

- The assignee tenant's references were unsatisfactory.
- The financial standing of the assignee is unsatisfactory.

In *Kened Ltd and Den Norske Bank plc* v *Connie Investments Ltd* (1997), Millett LJ said that the essential question is: 'Has it been shown that no reasonable landlord would have withheld consent?'

Note this following point in relation to leases granted on or after 1 January 1996:

Section 19(1A), Landlord and Tenant Act 1927 (added by Section 22, Landlord and Tenant (Covenants) Act 1995)

Landlord and tenant of a non-residential lease may agree in the lease what circumstances will justify the landlord in withholding or granting consent e.g. that the tenant enters an authorised guarantee agreement – see later.

Covenants in leases

Distinguish between:

- **express** covenants, i.e. actually contained in the lease;
- **implied** covenants, i.e. implied by law.

To be clear, covenants mean promises in a deed. Even where the lease is equitable (i.e. no deed), it is usual to talk of covenants.

Exam tip

- -

Typical examples of covenants in an exam question are: repairing, payment of rent, that the tenant will only use the premises for certain purposes. Exam questions will normally set these out as express covenants.

- -

Implied covenants are implied in the lease unless excluded – good ones to remember for the exam are:

- *Tenant's covenant to repair.* If the premises are in disrepair at the start of the lease then if the tenant covenants to 'keep them in repair' this means that he must put them in repair at his expense – *Payne* v *Haine* (1847).
- *Landlord's covenant for quiet enjoyment.* That is, that the tenant will not be disturbed by third-party rights and acts of the landlord which disturb possession, e.g. burst water

pipes causing water to flow into the premises. If this covenant is broken, there could also be liability for breach of section 1(3) of the Protection from Eviction Act 1977 – unlawful harassment.

Don't be tempted to . . .

A common exam question asks you about noise: this is a trap! Note Kekewich LJ in *Jenkins* v *Jackson* (1888), who observed that this covenant does not mean 'undisturbed by noise'. You will win marks here if you mention the judgments in *Southwark LBC* v *Mills* (2001), where the covenant was *not* broken by failure of the landlord to provide soundproofing in flats.

- *Landlord's covenants not to derogate from his grant,* i.e. not frustrate the purposes for which the premises were let such as interfering with a right to light. The covenant does not prevent the landlord setting up a competing business – *Port* v *Griffith* (1938).
- Under the Homes (Fitness for Human Habitation) Act 2018 there is an implied covenant in a lease that a landlord must ensure that the property is fit for human habitation at the beginning of the tenancy and for its duration; and where a landlord fails to do so, the tenant has the right to take action in the courts for breach of contract on the grounds that the property is unfit for human habitation. This is brought into force by inserting a new section 9A into the LTA 1985. This Act remedies a major gap in the law. Landlords were not previously required by implied covenant to ensure that properties they rented out were free of potentially harmful hazards from which a risk of harm might arise to the health or safety of the tenant or another occupier of the property. Now they are required to ensure this.

Impress your examiner

Ask if *Port* v *Griffith* would apply if the premises were to be let for a highly specialised purpose.

- *Tenant's covenant not to commit waste.* This means that 'the tenant must take proper care of the place' (Denning LJ in *Warren* v *Keen* (1954)).

Where there is doubt whether a covenant should be implied the test is that of Lord Hoffman in *Attorney-General of Belize* v *Belize Telecom Ltd* (2009): 'The court ... cannot introduce terms to make it fairer or more reasonable. It is concerned only to discover what the instrument means.'

We will come to the remedies for breaches of covenants a little later in this chapter.

Liability of the original landlord and tenant on the covenants

The original landlord and tenant are of course liable on the covenants while they are the actual landlord and tenant. When the freehold and the leasehold are assigned they may continue to be liable. This depends on whether the Landlord and Tenant (Covenants) Act 1995 applies. The Act applies to *all* leases granted on or after 1 January 1996 which by section 1(1) are referred to as 'new tenancies'. Pre-1 January 1996 tenancies are referred to as 'other tenancies'.

Note that by section 28(1) a 'new tenancy' includes an *agreement* for a tenancy, i.e. an equitable lease.

- If the legal (not equitable) lease was granted before 1 January 1996, both landlord and tenant remain liable on the covenants for the whole term of the lease even if they are no longer parties, i.e. the tenant has assigned the lease and the landlord has sold the freehold reversion. But see section 17, Landlord and Tenants (Covenants) Act 1995.
- If the lease was granted on or after 1 January 1996, then the Landlord and Tenant (Covenants) Act 1995 applies to legal and equitable leases.

Note that all the references to sections that follow are to sections of this Act.

Section 5, Landlord and Tenant (Covenants) Act 1995

The tenant on assigning the lease is released from his covenants and ceases to be entitled to the benefit of the landlord covenants.

However, the landlord may, as a condition of agreeing to the assignment, require the tenant to enter into an authorised guarantee agreement (AGA) (s. 16) guaranteeing that the incoming tenant will perform the covenants.

An AGA must exist before the tenant applies for licence to assign.

Example 6.2

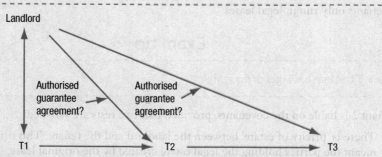

Landlord

Authorised guarantee agreement?

Authorised guarantee agreement?

T1 → T2 → T3

When the landlord gives consent to the assignment from T1 to T2, he can require T1 to enter an AGA under which T1 guarantees T2's liabilities under the lease. When T2 assigns to T3, the landlord may require T2 to enter into an AGA, but when the assignment is complete, T1's liability ends. This is a common exam point.

Section 6, Landlord and Tenant (Covenants) Act 1995

The landlord may, on selling the freehold reversion, be released from liability on his covenants. The procedure is set out in section 8.

Exam tip

Students often think that the date for deciding if the Landlord and Tenant (Covenants) Act 1995 applies is the date of the assignment of the lease. It is not. It is the date when the lease was originally granted.

Liability of the assignee landlord and tenant on the covenants

Once again, it is necessary to distinguish between pre-1 January 1996 and post-1 January 1996 leases:

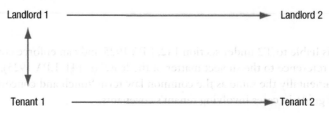

Landlord 1 → Landlord 2

Tenant 1 → Tenant 2

Pre-1 January 1996 leases

In this situation the distinction between legal and equitable leases is important as covenants only run in legal leases.

Exam tip

- -

Check if the lease is legal or equitable.

- -

Tenant 2 is liable on the covenants, provided that two tests are satisfied:

(1) There is 'privity of estate' between the landlord and the tenant. This originally meant the parties holding the legal estate created by the original lease, i.e. the original landlord and tenant. However, this principle has now been extended to assignee tenants (by common law) and assignee landlords (s. 141, LPA 1925 – see later).

(2) The covenants 'touch and concern the land' (*Spencer's Case* (1582)), e.g. covenants to pay the rent, user covenants, but not a covenant giving the tenant the right to purchase the freehold nor personal covenants.

Thomas v *Hayward* (1869) LR 4 Ex 311

Facts

The landlord of a public house covenanted that he would not open another 'beer or spirit house' within half a mile of the premises.

Legal principle

This did not bind an assignee tenant as it did not refer to anything to be done or not done on the premises.

Analysis

Although this decision is often quoted its correctness has been doubted: surely a covenant which benefits the business of the tenant should be capable of touching and concerning the land? This is the case with freehold covenants (Chapter 7). See *Newton Abbot Co-operative Society* v *Williams and Treadgold Ltd.* (1952). The same applies to easements – see Chapter 8 and *Moody* v *Steggles*.

Landlord 2 is liable to T2 under section 142, LPA 1925 and can enforce covenants which 'have reference to the subject matter of the lease' (s. 141, LPA 1925). This term means fundamentally the same as the common law term 'touch and concern' and is also a useful guide in cases involving tenant's covenants.

Post-1 January 1996 leases

The rules apply to both legal and equitable leases as we saw earlier.

Section 3, Landlord and Tenant (Covenants) Act 1995

'The benefit of all landlord and tenant covenants of a tenancy . . . shall in accordance with this section pass on an assignment of the whole or any part of the premises or of the reversion of them.'

Both incoming landlords and tenants are bound by covenants unless they are not landlord and tenant covenants, i.e. they are 'personal in character'. This is very similar to the old 'touch and concern' test.

Note that a question may involve breach by, for instance, a landlord of a covenant to repair and a refusal of the tenant in consequence to pay rent. Breach by one party does not excuse breach by the other and so the tenant is still liable to pay rent.

Don't be tempted to . . .

Make sure that you are clear about the liability of sub-tenants on a covenant in a lease. Remember these three points:

(1) There is no privity of estate between the landlord under the headlease and the sub-tenant (ST), i.e. the landlord is not a party to the sub-lease. This means that the landlord and the ST cannot directly enforce covenants against each other.

(2) The landlord can, as an exception to the above rule, enforce a restrictive covenant which is negative by an injunction against ST.

(3) The landlord can sue the tenant under the headlease for a breach of covenant committed by the sub-tenant and so claim to forfeit the lease – see next section in this chapter.

Example 6.3

There are two covenants in a lease:

(a) to repair the premises;

(b) not to use the premises for any purpose other than a high-class grocer's shop.

T has sub-let to ST. L can enforce covenant (b) against ST but can only enforce covenant (a) against T.

Remedies for breach of covenants

Tenant's remedies

Exam questions usually ask you about breaches of covenant by the tenant and so you need to concentrate on the landlord's remedies. In brief, the tenant's remedies are:

- damages, e.g. for breach of covenant by the landlord to repair;
- repudiation of the lease – possibly linked to a claim for damages;
- specific performance, e.g. *Posner* v *Scott-Lewis* (1986) – granted in respect of an obligation to employ a resident porter at a block of flats;
- appointment of a receiver, e.g. to make repairs.

Landlord's remedies

For breach of the covenant to pay rent

- Action for arrears of rent. Limited to six years' arrears: section 19, Limitation Act 1980.
- Forfeiture proceedings. This is the remedy which an exam question is most likely to ask you to deal with and you should approach it as shown in the diagram below.

Note: The remedy of distress was abolished by the Tribunals, Courts and Enforcement Act 2007. There is a replacement remedy for commercial leases.

For breaches of all other covenants

- Damages, e.g. for breach of the tenant's covenant to repair.
- Injunction, e.g. to prevent breaches of covenants.
- Forfeiture. Once again, an exam question may require you to deal with this in detail. Note carefully the differences in forfeiture here from forfeiture for non-payment of rent.

Impress your examiner

Exam questions often ask if a particular breach can be remedied. Consider this carefully.

The main case to mention here is *Expert Clothing Service and Sales Ltd* v *Hillgate House Ltd* (1987).

You may get a question where the tenant's use of the premises has cast a stigma over the premises, e.g. *Rugby School* v *Tannahill* (1935): use of premises for prostitution. Even if the use has ceased, the stigma may remain and so the breach cannot be remedied in a reasonable time.

Note: even if forfeiture proceedings succeed, a court order is still needed to evict a residential occupier – section 3(1), Protection from Eviction Act 1977. Occupier means any person lawfully residing in the premises and so includes licensees (sections 3(2A) and (2B)).

Exam tip

Point out the possible relevance of the ECHR in an eviction situation. (Check Chapter 1 for details.)

Impress your examiner

The Court of Appeal considered relief from forfeiture in three 2015 cases: *Magnic Ltd* v *Ul-Hassan*; *Safin (Fursecroft) Ltd* v *Badrig's Estate*; and *Freifeld* v *West Kensington Court Estate Ltd*. In each there were substantial breaches of covenants, as in *Freifeld* where lessees of a restaurant had, in breach of covenant, sublet the premises and their running of the restaurant was in breach of an 'anti-nuisance' covenant. However, relief from forfeiture was granted on terms that the lease be sold to a new tenant, with the approval of the landlord, within six months. See Duckworth and Sissons (2016) who review the obstacles in the way of landlords seeking forfeiture.

Forfeiture for non-payment of rent

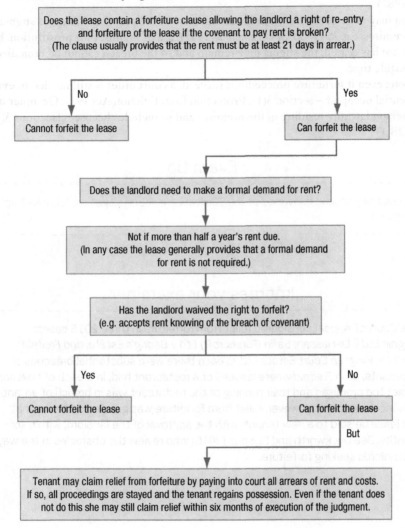

Does the lease contain a forfeiture clause allowing the landlord a right of re-entry and forfeiture of the lease if the covenant to pay rent is broken?
(The clause usually provides that the rent must be at least 21 days in arrear.)

No → Cannot forfeit the lease

Yes → Can forfeit the lease

Does the landlord need to make a formal demand for rent?

Not if more than half a year's rent due.
(In any case the lease generally provides that a formal demand for rent is not required.)

Has the landlord waived the right to forfeit?
(e.g. accepts rent knowing of the breach of covenant)

Yes → Cannot forfeit the lease

No → Can forfeit the lease

But

Tenant may claim relief from forfeiture by paying into court all arrears of rent and costs. If so, all proceedings are stayed and the tenant regains possession. Even if the tenant does not do this she may still claim relief within six months of execution of the judgment.

Forfeiture for other breaches

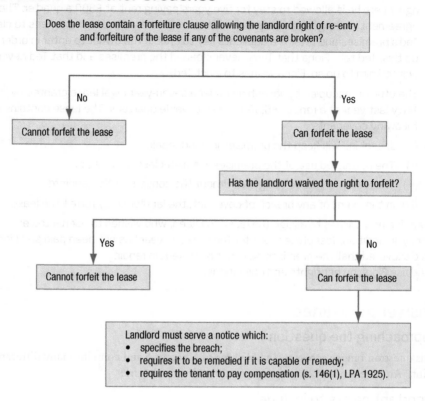

Does the lease contain a forfeiture clause allowing the landlord right of re-entry and forfeiture of the lease if any of the covenants are broken?

No → Cannot forfeit the lease

Yes → Can forfeit the lease

Has the landlord waived the right to forfeit?

Yes → Cannot forfeit the lease

No → Can forfeit the lease

Landlord must serve a notice which:
- specifies the breach;
- requires it to be remedied if it is capable of remedy;
- requires the tenant to pay compensation (s. 146(1), LPA 1925).

Putting it all together

Sample question

Could you answer this question? Following is a typical problem question that could arise on this topic. Additionally, a sample essay question and guidance on tackling it can be found on the companion website.

Problem question

Fiona has just purchased 155 High Street, Hanbury, a freehold registered property, consisting of a house and an adjoining office, from Terry.

(a) The top floor of the house is occupied by Ted under an agreement made two years ago where he is allowed to stay for five years paying rent at £300 a quarter. The agreement is unsigned and it provides that the owner of the house agrees to clean Ted's premises and retains a duplicate key to enable the owner to enter in order to do this. Ted tells Fiona that Terry never cleaned the premises and that Ted never wanted him to do so. Fiona wishes to evict Ted.

(b) The office is occupied by Josephine under a seven-year legal lease granted by Terry last year at a rent of £6,000 a year, payable quarterly. The lease contains the following covenants:

  (i) Josephine will keep the premises in good repair.

  (ii) The permitted use of the premises is a high-class retail shop.

  (iii) The lease cannot be assigned without the consent of the landlord.

  (iv) In the event of any breach of covenant, the landlord may forfeit the lease.

Josephine now wishes to assign the lease to Eileen, who wishes to open a travel agency. In addition, Josephine's rent for the previous year has not been paid and Fiona has discovered that the premises have not been kept in repair.

   Advise Fiona on her rights and obligations.

Answer guidelines

Approaching the question

This question ranges across the whole area of Chapter 6 and contains many different points. An excellent opportunity to score a really good mark!

Important points to include

(a) Lease or licence? Look at the three tests:

  (1) Exclusive possession?

  (2) Payment of rent?

  (3) Intention to create relationship of landlord and tenant?

If it could be a lease, is it for a definite term?
Could be a lease or a licence, so consider:

- If a licence, not binding on Fiona.
- If a lease, may bind Fiona, but first check:
  (i) What type of lease is it? Legal leases for more than three years should be created by deed (s. 54(2), LPA 1925). Is it an equitable lease? Apply *Walsh* v *Lonsdale* and section 2, Law of Property (Miscellaneous Provisions) Act 1989. As Ted is in occupation, he could have an overriding interest.
  (ii) If equitable, does it bind Fiona? Title is registered, so agreement could have been registered as an estate contract but does not seem to have been.

(iii) May be a periodical quarterly lease as rent has been paid. If so, it will count as an overriding interest (lease for less than seven years) and will bind Fiona.

(b) Lease was entered into after 1 January 1996, so the Landlord and Tenant (Covenants) Act 1995 will apply – counts as a 'new tenancy'.

Breach of repair and use covenant. Fiona may sue – section 141, LPA 1925.

Assignment of lease: section 19, Landlord and Tenant Act 1927 – can consent be withheld? Yes, as Eileen's proposed use is in breach of covenant.

Remedies of Fiona:

- damages;
- forfeiture – lease has forfeiture clause – procedure – apply section 146, LPA 1925 – can breaches be remedied? Discuss cases especially one of the recent CA ones.

Impress your examiner

- -

- Refer to the Law Commission's proposals in this area and to the recent CA cases.
- If there is an overriding interest, discuss whether it is actually binding by referring to Schedule 3, Paragraph 2 of the LRA 2002 (check Chapter 2).

Key case summary

Key case	How to use	Related topics
Street v *Mountford*	To state and explain the essential characteristics of a lease.	Leases contrasted with licences.
Antoniades v *Villiers*	To show that the use of the term 'licence' is not decisive: the courts look at the substance of the agreement.	Exclusive possession.
Mexfield Housing Co-operative Ltd v *Berrisford*	To show that leases must be of certain duration.	Formal requirements for the creation of leases.
Walsh v *Lonsdale*	To show that alongside legal leases it is also possible to have an equitable lease.	Legal and equitable leases.

▶

Key case	How to use	Related topics
No.1 West India Quay (Residential) Ltd v *East Tower Apartments Ltd*	To explain the grounds when it is reasonable for a landlord to refuse consent to the assignment of a lease.	Assignments of leases.
Thomas v *Hayward*	To illustrate when a leasehold covenant may 'touch and concern' the land.	Liability of tenants on covenants.

Key further reading

Key articles/reports	How to use	Related topics
Baker, A. (2014) *Bruton*, licensees in possession and a fiction of title. 6 *Conv.* 495.	This looks at the *Bruton* decision and argues for the idea that consensual possession is a root of title. This challenges orthodox thinking and so is excellent in giving you that different angle in an essay question which earns you extra marks.	Nature of a lease.
Pascoe, S. (2018) Periodic tenancies subject to a fetter on the tenant – doctrinal dilemmas? 2 *Conv.* 119.	This interesting article looks at the decision in *Mexfield* from a different angle to the usual one: does the *Mexfield* principle imposing a grant of a 90-year lease subject to the terms of the original agreement also apply in the same way to a fetter on the tenant?	Requirement that a lease must be for a term certain.
Duckworth, N. and Sissons, P. (2016) Forfeiture revisited: Magnic, Safin and Freifeld 4 *Conv.* 286.	This looks at the present law on forfeiture of leases by the landlord, an area widely felt to be in need of reform. See also, the Law Commission Report.	Landlords' remedies for breach of tenants' covenants.

Key articles/reports	How to use	Related topics
Sissons, P. (2018) *No.1 West India Quay (Residential) Ltd* v *East Tower Apartments Ltd* [2018] EWCA Civ 250 (CA). 3 *Conv.* 296.	This looks at the interpretation of the term 'reasonableness' by the CA in this case and asks if it is appropriate to apply public law principles to the exercise of a contractual discretion, as here.	Assignments of leases.
Whayman, D. (2019) Old issues, new incentives, new approach? Property guardians and the lease/licence distinction. 1 *Conv.* 47	This looks at cases where property guardian companies have taken disused buildings, converted them into residential units and rented them out to 'guardians' – private individuals – under a licence to prevent squatting until the owner wants the building back. The status of a licence has been challenged in recent cases.	Lease/licence distinction.

go.pearson.com/uk/lawexpress

Go online to access more revision support including quizzes to test your knowledge, sample questions with answer guidelines, printable versions of the topic maps, and more!

7

Covenants affecting freehold land

Revision checklist

Essential points you should know:

- Positive and negative covenants
- Liability of the original covenantor
- When section 56(1) of the LPA 1925 could apply
- Rules on when the benefit of a restrictive covenant may run
- Rules on when the burden of a restrictive covenant may run at common law
- The remedies for breach of a restrictive covenant
- Law Commission proposals for reform

Topic map

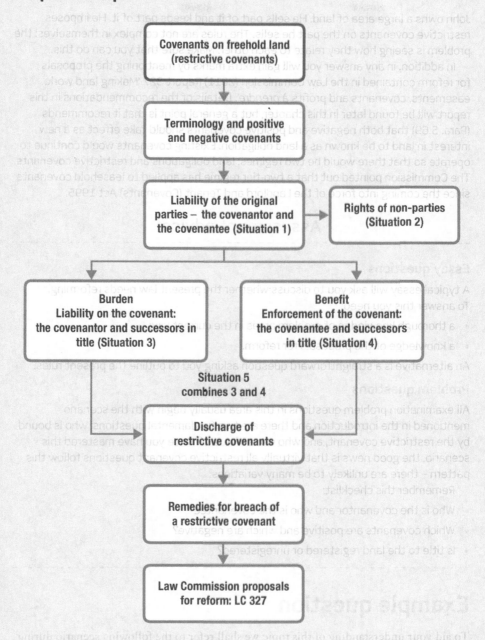

Covenants on freehold land (restrictive covenants)

↓

Terminology and positive and negative covenants

↓

Liability of the original parties – the covenantor and the covenantee (Situation 1) → **Rights of non-parties (Situation 2)**

↓

Burden
Liability on the covenant: the covenantor and successors in title (Situation 3)

Benefit
Enforcement of the covenant: the covenantee and successors in title (Situation 4)

Situation 5 combines 3 and 4

↓

Discharge of restrictive covenants

↓

Remedies for breach of a restrictive covenant

↓

Law Commission proposals for reform: LC 327

A printable version of this topic map is available from **go.pearson.com/uk/lawexpress**

Introduction

John owns a large area of land. He sells part of it and keeps part of it. He imposes restrictive covenants on the part he sells. The rules are not complex in themselves: the problem is seeing how they relate to each other. Make sure that you can do this.

In addition, in any answer you will gain extra marks by mentioning the proposals for reform contained in the Law Commission (2011) Report 327 'Making land work: easements, covenants and profits à prendre'. Details of the recommendations in this report will be found later in this chapter, but a general point is that it recommends (Para. 5.69) that both negative and positive covenants should take effect as a new interest in land to be known as a land obligation. Existing covenants would continue to operate so that there would be two regimes: land obligations and restrictive covenants. The Commission pointed out that a two-tier regime has applied to leasehold covenants since the coming into force of the Landlord and Tenant (Covenants) Act 1995.

Assessment advice

Essay questions

A typical essay will ask you to discuss whether the present law needs reforming. To answer this you need:

- a thorough knowledge of problem areas in the current law;
- a knowledge of the proposals for reform.

An alternative is a straightforward question asking you to outline the present rules.

Problem questions

All examination problem questions in this area usually begin with the scenario mentioned in the introduction and there are two fundamental questions: who is bound by the restrictive covenant, and who can enforce it? Once you have mastered this scenario, the good news is that virtually all restrictive covenant questions follow this pattern – there are unlikely to be many variations.

Remember this checklist:

- Who is the covenantor and who is the covenantee?
- Which covenants are positive and which are negative?
- Is title to the land registered or unregistered?

Example question

To aid your understanding of this topic we shall refer to the following scenario during this chapter.

In 2016 Michael, who owned 'Pinetrees', an estate of 10,000 acres with registered freehold title, sold off 'The Laurels' a house with one acre of ground attached, on the edge of the estate, to Susan. In the transfer Susan covenanted:

(a) Not to carry on a business from 'The Laurels'.

(b) To keep all fences, hedges and walls forming the boundary of 'The Laurels' in good repair.

(c) Not to keep any pets on 'The Laurels'.

(d) To contribute to the upkeep of the drains which service the whole of Michael's estate, including 'The Laurels'.

Susan also entered into the same covenants with 'the owners of land now or formerly part of Pinetrees'.

In 2017 Michael sold another house, 'Firtrees' on the far side of the estate, to Arthur.

In 2019 Susan sold 'The Laurels' to Aidan. Aidan is proposing to run his accountants' practice from 'The Laurels', he keeps a pet alligator and he refuses to contribute to the upkeep of the drains. Meanwhile the hedges are overgrown and Aidan has not cut them back.

Advise Michael and Arthur on any right of action which they may have in respect of the breaches of covenants.

Covenants on freehold land (definitions)

Covenants on freehold land

Covenants are promises contained in deeds and, as a transfer of the freehold title to land must be by deed (s. 52(1), LPA 1925), Susan's promises to Michael in the scenario are called covenants.

Restrictive covenants

A restrictive covenant is a type of covenant which restricts the use of land (e.g. it provides that the land shall not be built on). The word 'restrictive' in this topic is, in fact, misleading, although the term will be used in this chapter as it is so commonly used.

Positive and negative covenants

Covenants on land are of two types: positive and negative.

Negative covenants are those which restrict the use to which the land may be put. The simplest test for distinguishing between positive and negative covenants is to ask if performance of them requires expenditure of money.

Exam tip

Knowing the distinction between positive and negative covenants is vital to answering a question on this area.

Covenants which 'touch and concern the land' and personal covenants

The former phrase has been met before in Chapter 6 on leases and it means that the covenant must benefit the land itself. The real point is that the covenant must not be personal, e.g. 'to do X's shopping for him'. The importance of this distinction will become clear when we look at covenant (c) from the earlier scenario.

The parties involved

The person who agrees to the covenant is the *covenantor* and the person with whom the agreement is made is the *covenantee*. The covenantor will usually be the buyer of the land because the seller will have required the buyer to agree to the covenants as a condition of the sale. In our example Susan is the covenantor and Michael is the covenantee.

Exam tip

Your first step in answering a problem question on covenants should always be to identify the covenantor and covenantee.

Benefit and burden

Land to which the covenant applies is *burdened* by the covenant and this will be land owned by the *covenantor*. Land owned by the *covenantee* is *benefited* by the covenant. Thus in our earlier question 'The Laurels', owned by Susan , is the burdened land and 'Pinetrees', owned by Michael, is the benefited land.

Registered and unregistered title to land

Note that this chapter only deals with covenants on freehold land; leasehold covenants are dealt with in Chapter 6. It is a good idea at this point to return to Chapter 2 and check that you know how restrictive covenants fit into the scheme of registered and unregistered land.

Exam questions will be most unlikely to mix up freehold and leasehold covenants. In short, the message is not to worry about leasehold covenants for now!

There are *five basic situations* that occur with restrictive covenants, and problems in an examination will revolve around these. The following figure illustrates these (note: 'Situation two' is not shown here).

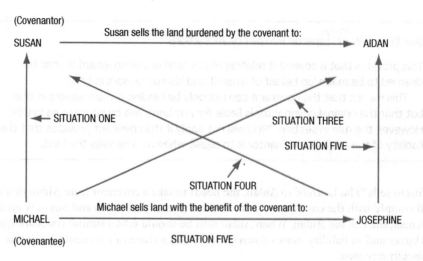

Situation one: liability of the original parties – the covenantor and the covenantee

Michael the original covenantee and Susan is the original covenantor. Suppose that Susan is in breach of the covenants.

(a) The original parties can claim against each other on the covenant, so Michael (the covenantee) can claim against (Susan) (the covenantor).

In this situation, Michael can sue Susan on the covenants. As between the original parties, all covenants are binding, which means that this basic rule applies to all covenants.

When the rights of subsequent parties are involved, the law distinguishes between different types of covenants.

(b) The original covenantor may continue to be liable on the covenant even though he/she is no longer the owner of the land. This rule is not only one of common law but is also implied by section 79(1), LPA 1925.

Section 79(1), Law of Property Act 1925

This provides that a covenant relating to any land of the covenantor shall be deemed to be made 'on behalf of himself and his successors in title'.

This means that the covenant can not only be binding on successors in title but that the original covenantor is liable for any breaches by successors in title. However, the rule in section 79(1) will not apply if the covenant provides that the liability of the original covenantor is to cease when he/she sells the land.

If Susan sells 'The Laurels' to Aidan, she needs to take a covenant from Aidan that he will comply with the covenants. Then, if Aidan does breach them and Susan is sued by Michael, she can sue Aidan. When Aidan sells he should take a similar covenant from his buyer and so liability moves down the line with a chain of covenants, known as *indemnity covenants*.

Situation two: rights of non-parties

This is the same scenario as 'Situation one' but with an addition:

Susan enters into the same covenants as she entered into with Michael with 'the owners of land now or formerly part of Pinetrees'. This means that she has covenanted with the owners of land (Firtrees) adjacent to Michael's land (Pinetrees), in this case Arthur.

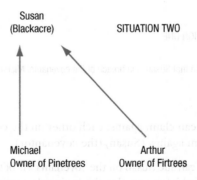

Susan
(Blackacre)

SITUATION TWO

Michael
Owner of Pinetrees

Arthur
Owner of Firtrees

The right of Arthur to enforce the covenant is contained in section 56(1) of the LPA 1925.

Section 56(1), Law of Property Act 1925

'A person may take . . . the benefit of any condition, right of entry, covenant or agreement over or respecting land or other property, although he may not be named as a party to the conveyance or other instrument.'

Thus in our scenario – where the provision regarding adjacent landowners is spelt out in the covenant – section 56(1) would allow adjacent owners of land to sue. If there wasn't such a clause in our scenario, section 56(1) would not apply.

Exam tip

In any exam question ask if the person seeking to enforce the benefit of the covenant was in existence at the time the covenant was made. If the answer is yes, then he or she may be able to enforce the covenant subject to the following test.

See *Re Ecclesiastical Commissioners Conveyance* (1936).

Neuberger J in *Amsprop Trading Ltd* v *Harris Distribution Ltd* (1997): 'The true aim of section 56 seems to be not to allow a third party to sue on a contract merely because it is for his benefit; *the contract must purport to be made with him*', i.e. does the covenantor actually promise the covenantee that owners of adjacent land will benefit?

Section 1, Contracts (Rights of Third Parties) Act 1999

Section 1 enables a person who is not a party to a contract to take the benefit of a contractual term which purports to confer a benefit on him.

This Act covers the whole of the law of contract, not just this area; but in this area this Act and section 56(1) of the LPA overlap.

This wording clearly applies to our situation as the covenant is contained in a contract and it confers a benefit on third parties, i.e. Arthur as an adjoining landowner. Thus, it can be seen how section 56(1) of the LPA and this Act overlap, and a good answer would explain that either could be used.

It is possible to have wording which would allow Arthur to claim under the Contracts (Rights of Third Parties) Act 1999 but not under section 56(1): 'this covenant is entered into with the owners of *all* land adjoining Pinetrees', rather than the owners of land '*now or formerly* forming part of Pinetrees'. It could be argued that this could include Arthur if he acquired Firtrees *after* Susan entered into the covenants whereas section 56(1) would not apply.

Exam tip

Look carefully at the exact wording of the covenant and see to whom it applies.

Situation three: liability on the covenant – the covenantor and successors in title

Common law and equity

Equity goes further than the common law in allowing the enforcement of covenants between successors in title of the original parties. The common law and equitable rules do not overlap and so the fact that they are mutually exclusive means that examination answers must carefully distinguish between them.

Situation three in detail

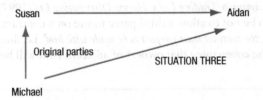

The starting position is scenario one, with Susan and Michael as the original covenantor and covenantee. However, Susan now sells to Aidan. Michael remains the owner of Pinetrees. Assume that Aidan is in breach of all the covenants. Can Michael bring an action against Aidan?

This section will consider in each case whether the *burden* of the covenant has passed to Aidan.

The answers are different in each case but initially we can leave covenant (c) until later and deal with (a) and (b).

Covenants (a) and (b)

The first thing that you should do with this situation is consider which of the covenants are *positive* and which are *negative*. The covenant in (a) is negative.

The distinction between positive and negative covenants is vital because positive covenants generally only bind the original covenantor, i.e. Susan in our scenario, and not subsequent parties, i.e. Aidan. However, in equity generally negative covenants can bind subsequent parties.

Exam tip

These rules will usually appear in a problem question on covenants.

* Positive covenants, with only a few exceptions, only bind the original parties.
* Negative covenants can bind subsequent parties in equity.

The rules on positive covenants in more detail

The common law rule on positive covenants was established in *Austerberry* v *Oldham Corporation* (1885) where it was held that at common law positive covenants do not bind subsequent owners of land (followed in *Rhone* v *Stephens* (1994)). Applied to 'Situation three', this means that positive covenant (b) to keep all fences in repair *is not* binding on Aidan.

Note that in a survey of 315 deeds Walsh and Morris (2015) found that 41 per cent referred to positive covenants as distinct from negative and the most common positive covenants were to contribute to maintenance of a fence, a shared accessway and to the appearance of property.

Exam tip

A simple way to distinguish between positive and negative covenants is to ask if the covenant requires the spending of money. If so, it is likely to be positive.

The rules on negative covenants in more detail

Equity takes a different view on *negative* covenants, as established in the following case:

Tulk v *Moxhay* (1848) Ph 774 (CA)

Facts
There was a covenant not to build on land in the middle of Leicester Square in London.

Legal principle
It was held that it was binding on a subsequent purchaser of that land and so restrictive covenants take effect as an equitable interest in land.

Analysis
The actual decision did not refer to negative covenants but simply held that in equity, a covenant can bind subsequent owners, on certain conditions. This rule was refined in subsequent cases so that it only applied to negative covenants – see *Haywood* v *Brunswick Permanent Benefit Building Society* (1881). The court in *Tulk* based its decision on the fact that the purchaser had notice of it but the later cases have concentrated on the content of the covenant: was it positive or negative?

Applied to our situation, and provided that the conditions set out below are satisfied, the negative covenant (a) not to carry on a business *is* binding on Aidan.

The term 'notice' has a particular meaning in land law, and if you are still uncertain what it means, revise this now by referring back to Chapter 1.

If the covenant is negative, the following other conditions must be satisfied before equity will enforce it against subsequent parties:

(a) The covenantee must own land for the benefit of which the covenant was entered into. See *LCC* v *Allen* (1914).

(b) *The covenant must touch and concern the dominant land.* As mentioned earlier, the point here is the covenant must not be personal.

(c) *It must be the common intention of the parties that the covenant shall run.* Covenants made on or after 1 January 1926 are deemed to be made with subsequent parties (s. 79, LPA 1925). Covenants made before that date will run if the language indicates this, e.g. 'the covenant is made by the covenantor for himself, his heirs and assigns'.

(d) *The covenantee must have notice of the covenant.*

   (i) If title to the burdened land is registered, the covenant must be protected by a notice on the register of that title (s. 29, LRA 2002). If it is not, the covenant will not bind a purchaser.

   (ii) If title to the land is not registered and the covenant was entered into on or after 1 January 1926, it must be registered as a Class D(ii) land charge; otherwise it will not bind a purchaser.

   (iii) If title to the land is not registered and the covenant was entered into before 1 January 1926, the old notice rules apply and the covenant will not bind a purchaser unless he/she has notice of it (see Chapter 2 for a discussion of notice).

In effect, registration under (i) and (ii) constitutes notice.

Note: if the covenant was not registered when Aidan bought The Laurels, it would not bind him. However, it could be registered after he bought it, and if Aidan sold The Laurels to, for example, Charles it would bind Charles.

Covenant (c)

This the covenant not to keep any pets on 'The Laurels'.

It could be argued that this is a personal covenant as it does not benefit the land but in fact such a covenant is generally held to actually benefit the land and so the answer would be the same as for covenant (a) earlier and would bind Aidan. The alligator will have to go!

Covenant (d)

This is a covenant by the owner of Pinetrees to contribute to the maintenance of the sewers which serve *both* Pinetrees and The Laurels. As such, it is a positive covenant and so it would not be enforceable against subsequent owners of Pinetrees were it not for a special rule.

Covenants of this kind operate in situations where there are reciprocal benefits and burdens enjoyed by users of the facility. A mention of such a covenant in an examination question should lead you to mention this case:

Halsall v Brizell [1957] 1 All ER 371 (HC)

Facts
Buyers of building plots covenanted to contribute to the cost of repairs of sewers and roads that were for the common use of the owners of all the building plots.

Legal principle
An agreement to contribute to the cost of these repairs was binding on a subsequent owner, on the principle that you cannot take the benefit of these rights yet avoid the burdens of them.

Analysis
The rule that positive covenants do not bind successors in title has to some extent been mitigated by the 'benefit and burden' principle in this case. Bevan (2018) notes that Upjohn LJ did not elaborate any rationale for the doctrine beyond remarking that its existence was 'conceded' and so the effect is that the doctrine is based on what Bevan calls 'broad and clichéd notions of fairness, of not having one's cake and eating it'.

One obvious example of where this principle applies is an agreement to contribute to the cost of maintenance of a shared drive or private road. In *Rhone* v *Stephens* (1994) Lord Templeman said that it would *not* apply when the owner had no choice whether to accept both the benefit and the burden. It is probably on this basis that mutual covenants between neighbours to maintain a fence between their respective properties would not come under *Halsall* v *Brizell*.

Impress your examiner

Look at the judgment of Peter Gibson LJ in *Thamesmead Town Ltd* v *Allotey* (1998) for a detailed consideration of when the *Halsall* v *Brizell* principle can apply.

The Law Commission has recommended (LC 327 (2011) at Para. 5.69) that existing rules on negative and positive covenants on freehold land should be replaced by a new land obligation which would be a legal interest in land and would include both positive and negative covenants and therefore subsequent parties would be bound. It would operate in broadly the same way as an easement with a requirement for both a dominant and servient tenement but would not be retrospective. There would be a requirement, as at present, that the benefit of the obligation would have to touch and concern the benefited land. Land obligations could only be created expressly. Where title is registered the benefit and burden would have to be registered and if title is unregistered the burden (but not the benefit) would be registrable as a land charge (Para. 6.57).

One issue is exactly how a positive land obligation would be enforced: proceedings for specific performance, damages or self-help, e.g. if an obligation to repair a fence is broken the covenantee simply repairs it and charges the covenantor. See Walsh and Morris (2015).

Impress your examiner

It is too easy to just say that the law should be simplified so that there are the same rules for positive and negative covenants. Look at a critical view in O'Connor (2011) who writes from a comparative perspective.

Situation four: enforcing the benefit at common law – the covenantee and successors in title

Suppose now that we add to the scenario so that Michael sells Pinetrees to Josephine but Susan remains the owner of The Laurels. Can Josephine bring an action against Susan? This involves the question of whether the *benefit* of the covenant has passed to Josephine.

We have already seen in 'Situation one' that the covenantee (Michael) can enforce the covenants against the covenantor (Susan). We are now looking at whether successors in title to the covenantee can enforce the covenant, i.e. in our situation, whether Josephine can enforce the covenant. Remember that this will be enforcing the *benefit* of the covenant.

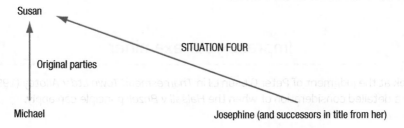

Note what was said in the introduction to 'Situation three': common law and equity take different approaches and do not mix. The common law will allow Josephine, provided that certain conditions are met (see list that follows), to enforce the covenants against Susan. This only applies to actions against *the original covenantor*.

Note here that equitable rules will apply when we come to consider, in 'Situation five', what happens when Susan sells The Laurels to Aidan.

The following conditions must be met for Josephine to able to show that the benefit of the covenant has passed to her and that she can sue Susan for breach of them:

(a) The covenant *must touch and concern the land* (*Rogers v Hosegood* (1900)). See earlier under 'Situation three' for an explanation of this term.

(b) The original covenantee must have had a legal estate in the land which is benefited.

(c) The successor in title (Josephine) must have also acquired a legal estate in the land.

(d) The benefit of the covenant was intended by the original parties to run with the land.

Smith and Snipes Hall Farm v River Douglas Catchment Board (1949) is a good illustration of this area.

Situation five: enforcing the benefit in equity – successors in title to both covenantee and covenantor

Michael sells Pinetrees to Josephine; Susan sells The Laurels to Aidan. Aidan is in breach of all the standard covenants. Can Josephine bring an action against Aidan? This involves whether the *benefit* has passed to Josephine and the burden has *passed* to Aidan.

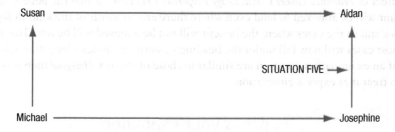

Note that the rules in 'Situation four' are of no help at all where Josephine wishes to sue Aidan. If Josephine is to have a right to enforce against Aidan, then this can only be in equity because, as we saw in 'Situation three', Aidan is only liable in equity.

There are three methods under which Josephine can show that the benefit of a covenant has passed to her *in equity*. By:

(a) annexation;

(b) assignment; or

(c) proof of the existence of a building scheme.

Annexation

The benefit of the covenant is *attached to the land*, glued to it, in effect. Whoever acquires title to the land benefited by the covenant (the dominant land) also acquires the benefit of the covenant.

This can happen by:

- **Express annexation.** Look at the words of the deed which created the covenant. In an exam question you may be given the actual words in a conveyance and asked if they amount to an express annexation. Contrast the words used in *Rogers* v *Hosegood* (1900) and *Renals* v *Cowlishaw* (1878).

- **Implied annexation.** This is where there is no mention in the covenant that it benefits particular land and so any intention to annexe the benefit of covenant to the land must be implied. See *Marten* v *Flight Refuelling Ltd* (1962).

- **Statutory annexation.**

Section 78(1), Law of Property Act 1925

'A covenant relating to the land of the covenantee shall be deemed to be made with the covenantee and his successors in title.'

This includes all covenants which relate to the land but will not include personal covenants, e.g. 'to do X's shopping for her'.

The effect of *Federated Homes* v *Mill Lodge Properties Ltd* (1980) is that the benefit of a covenant will be annexed to land even where there are no words of the kind in *Rogers* v *Hosegood* and so the cases where the benefit will not be annexed will be few. This means that most cases will now fall under the heading of statutory annexation, although if the facts of an examination question are similar to those of *Rogers* v *Hosegood* then it is as well to treat it as express annexation.

Impress your examiner

- -

Federated Homes has not escaped criticism. Look at, e.g., Newsome (1982) Universal Annexation 98 (LQR) 202.

Assignment

Its importance was diminished by *Federated Homes* which has made annexation the method of transferring the benefit of a covenant in the great majority of cases.

Roake v *Chadha* (1983) is a good example.

By proof of the existence of a building scheme

This is often found in practice.

Example 7.1

Michael, instead of selling part of his land to Susan, decides to develop it all and to sell it in individual plots with houses on each plot. Michael wants the area to be kept tidy and to remain residential, as this will affect the price which he will be able to obtain for each plot. Therefore, he requires each buyer to enter the following covenants with both the developers and with all other owners:

(a) not to run a business from their house;

(b) not to erect any fences, walls, hedges, etc., in their front gardens.

The effect is to create a local law for that area and, provided that the requirements for a building scheme are satisfied, then these covenants are enforceable.

See *Elliston* v *Reacher* (1908) for an example of the operation of a building scheme and *Birdlip Ltd* v *Hunter* (2016) for a recent instance of where there was insufficient evidence of one.

These requirements have been relaxed in some cases (see, e.g., *Baxter v Four Oaks Properties* Ltd (1965)), but the essential feature remains: there must have been a common intention that the purchaser would be subject to mutual restrictions which are reciprocal, i.e. a local law.

Summary of situation five

The effect of combining the rule that a party can be bound in equity by a negative covenant (Aidan) with the rule that in equity a party can claim the benefit of a covenant (Josephine) is that Josephine can sue Aidan for breach of the covenant not to run a business on The Laurels.

Discharge of covenants

Section 84(1), Law of Property Act 1925

The Lands Chamber has power 'wholly or partly to discharge or modify' a restrictive covenant.

There are several grounds for this: for instance, that the covenant is obsolete, that it impedes reasonable use of the land, that the removal of the covenant would not injure those entitled to any benefit, or that they have agreed to the removal of the covenant. Compensation may be ordered to be paid to the person(s) entitled to the benefit of the covenant which was discharged or modified. *Re Lynch* (2016) is a good recent example of the operation of section 84(1).

The Law Commission Report (LC 327) has recommended that the jurisdiction of the Lands Chamber to discharge or modify a restrictive covenant under section 84(1) of the LPA 1925 would also apply to land obligations and the grounds for the exercise of this jurisdiction would be made more transparent. It proposes a special provision to deal with possible discharge of positive covenants (which it proposes can now be enforced against non-parties) and that the Lands Chamber can modify a positive land obligation if, through changes in circumstances, performance of it has ceased to be reasonably practicable or has become unreasonably expensive as compared with the benefit (Para. 7.69). The Queen's Speech setting out the Government's legislative proposals for the 2016–17 session promised a Law of Property Bill to give effect to these recommendations but at the time of writing (October 2019) there has been no further news of this Bill.

See Lugger (2014) who considers whether a removal of a restrictive covenant under section 84 can be a breach of Article 1 of the First Protocol to the European Convention on Human Rights.

Putting it all together

Remedies for breach of a restrictive covenant

- Injunction.
- Damages in lieu of an injunction.

Exam tip

Do not forget to mention remedies at the end of your answer. Students often do forget and lose marks.

Sample question

Could you answer this question? What follows is a typical problem question that could arise on this topic. Additionally, a sample essay question and guidance on tackling it can be found on the companion website.

Problem question

John owns a large area of land. He sells part of it, Blackacre, to Rosemary and keeps part of it, Whiteacre, on which he has a house. He imposes restrictive covenants on the part he sells. The covenants are:

(a) that no business shall be carried on at Blackacre;

(b) that all fences must be kept in repair;

(c) that the owner of Blackacre shall contribute to the maintenance of the sewers which serve both Blackacre and Whiteacre.

These covenants are expressed to be for the benefit of Whiteacre.

Rosemary subsequently sells Blackacre to Aidan, and John sells Whiteacre to Eileen. Aidan has decided to run his accountancy business from Blackacre and is seeking planning permission from the local authority to enable him to do this. He has failed to repair the fences and he refuses to contribute to the maintenance of the sewers.

Advise Eileen on any action which she may take against Aidan to enforce the covenants. Title to both Blackacre and Whiteacre is registered.

Answer guidelines

Approaching the question

Do not be afraid of problem questions on this area. A calm, logical approach will get you good marks.

Important points to include

Action by Eileen against Aidan. Eileen must prove that:

- her land has the benefit of the covenants;
- Aidan's land has the burden of the covenants.

Consider Aidan first:

- **Covenant (a):** negative (*Tulk* v *Moxhay*) so burden may pass – go through conditions for this to happen (*LCC* v *Allen*, etc.) and note also that the covenants must be registered. The question says that title to the land is registered and so answer for only registered land. If the question does not say whether it is registered then answer for both registered and unregistered land.
- **Covenant (b):** positive (*Austerberry* v *Oldham Corporation*), so Aidan cannot be bound, although Rosemary remains liable on the covenant.
- **Covenant (c):** *Halsall* v *Brizell* situation.

Now consider Eileen.

- Eileen can sue Aidan under (a) if the benefit has passed to her in equity. The covenants are expressed to be made for the benefit of Whiteacre so this may be enough (see *Rogers* v *Hosegood*) but, in any case, on the basis of *Federated Homes* (applying section 78(1) of the LPA 1925) there is probably statutory annexation.
- Aidan not liable under (b).
- Eileen can sue Aidan under (c) under the benefit–burden principle.

Finally, do not forget remedies: injunction plus damages?

Impress your examiner

Look at each of these points:

- Uncertainty if *Halsall* v *Brizell* applies, note case law.
- Mention Law Commission proposals for reform – look at what the answer would be if these proposals were implemented.

Key case summary

Key case	How to use	Related topics
Tulk v *Moxhay*	To show that negative freehold covenants run with the land in equity (but not common law) on certain conditions.	Covenants in equity.
Halsall v *Brizell*	To explain that there is an exceptional situation where a positive covenant may bind subsequent owners.	Positive covenants at common law.

Key further reading

Key articles/reports	How to use	Related topics
Law Commission (2011) Report 327, Making land work: easements, covenants and profits *à prendre*.	This has a host of proposals to reform this area of the law. Although they have yet to be implemented it is likely that at some stage they will be and so you need to know the thinking behind them.	Restrictive covenants. Easements. Profits.
Lugger, A. (2014) Daylight robbery: is the removal of a restrictive covenant under section 84 of the Law of Property Act 1925 a breach of human rights? 6 *Conv*. 507.	Students often ignore the applicability of s.84 of the LPA in questions on restrictive covenants. In fact, it is very important in practice and this article gives an interesting angle on this area.	Removal/ modification of restrictive covenants.
Bevan C. (2018) The doctrine of benefit and burden: reforming the law of covenants and the numerous clauses 'problem'. 77(1) *CLJ* 72.	This article looks at the 'benefit and burden' principle and at the decision in *Halsall v Brizell*. It looks at recent cases on this area and highlights the case for reform.	Passing of the burden in restrictive covenants.
O'Connor, P. (2011) Careful what you wish for: positive freehold covenants. 3 *Conv*. 191.	This article has a more critical view than is usually taken of the proposals to have the same rules for the enforceability of both positive and negative covenants.	Questions on possible reform of this area of the law.
Walsh, E. and Morris, C. (2015) Enforcing positive covenants: a practical perspective. 4 *Conv*. 316.	This article has some really excellent research detail on positive and negative covenants in practice.	Questions on positive and negative covenants.

go.pearson.com/uk/lawexpress

Go online to access more revision support including quizzes to test your knowledge, sample questions with answer guidelines, printable versions of the topic maps, and more!

8

Easements and profits

Revision checklist

Essential points you should know:

- What is an easement and what is a profit
- Characteristics of easements and profits
- When an easement and a profit is a legal interest and when an equitable interest
- How easements and profits can be created
- How rules on profits differ from easements
- Law Commission proposals for reform

Topic map

```
                    ┌─────────────────────────────────────┐
                    │ Easements and profits distinguished  │
                    └─────────────────────────────────────┘
                                    │
                    ┌─────────────────────────────────────┐
                    │      Characteristics of easements    │
                    └─────────────────────────────────────┘
                                    │
    ┌───────────────────────────────────────────────────────────────────┐
    │  Dominant/servient      Diversity of ownership      Subject of grant │
    │      tenement                                                        │
    │                                                                     │
    │              Accommodates the dominant tenement                     │
    └───────────────────────────────────────────────────────────────────┘
                                    │
    ┌──────────────────┐    ┌─────────────────────────────────────┐
    │ Note car parking │◄───│  If these satisfied then can be an easement │
    └──────────────────┘    └─────────────────────────────────────┘
                                    │
                    ┌─────────────────────────────────────┐
                    │  Is the easement legal or equitable? │
                    └─────────────────────────────────────┘
                                    │
                    ┌─────────────────────────────────────┐
                    │   Methods of creation of easements   │
                    └─────────────────────────────────────┘
                                    │
        ┌───────────────────┬───────────────┬───────────────────┐
  ┌──────────────┐   ┌──────────────┐   ┌──────────────┐
  │ Express grant│   │ Implication  │   │ Prescription │
  └──────────────┘   └──────────────┘   └──────────────┘
                                                │
                                      ┌─────────────────────┐
                                      │   Three methods      │
                                      │   of prescription    │
                                      └─────────────────────┘

                    ┌─────────────────────────────────────┐
                    │              Profits                 │
                    └─────────────────────────────────────┘

                    ┌─────────────────────────────────────┐
                    │        Law Commission                │
                    │     proposals for reform:            │
                    │            LC 327                    │
                    └─────────────────────────────────────┘
```

A printable version of this topic map is available from **go.pearson.com/uk/lawexpress**

Introduction

Questions are usually on easements but watch for one on a profit, e.g. on grazing rights.

Watch for a possible connection with licences (Chapter 5) and with land registration (Chapter 2). The basic principles are fairly straightforward but do watch for tricky areas such as the application of the rule in *Wheeldon* v *Burrows* and the grant of easements under section 62 of the LPA 1925. In addition, in any answer you will gain extra marks by mentioning the proposals for reform contained in the Law Commission (2011) Report 327, 'Making land work: easements, covenants and profits *à prendre*', which are referred to in this chapter. These will be given statutory force if and when the Law of Property Bill 2016, becomes law and you should watch for when this happens.

Assessment advice

Essay questions

This is a good subject for essays. Topics include:

- Can new negative easements be created?
- Rules on the grant of implied easements, especially the ambit of section 62 of the LPA 1925.
- Possible reform of the law on acquisition of easements by prescription. This is still very topical in view of the Law Commission Report – see Introduction.

Problem questions

Problem questions usually follow a familiar pattern which requires you to deal with the following areas. You must address all of these issues:

- Can the right be an easement or a profit at all? At this stage you may eliminate some of the rights which may be only licences.
- If it is, is it legal or equitable? This will involve you in considering the third point:
- Was it correctly created?

Easements and profits distinguished

Similarities: Both easements and profits (in full, *profits à prendre*) are proprietary interests in land.

Differences: Easements are rights over the land of another, e.g. rights to light, rights of way.

Profits are rights to enter on the land of another and take the profits of it.

This chapter now deals mainly with easements and looks at profits at the end. This is because you are more likely to get exam questions on easements.

Characteristics of easements

These are from *Re Ellenborough Park* (1955).

A dominant and a servient tenement

The easement must benefit land and there must be two pieces of land:

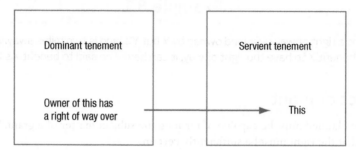

Diversity of ownership

The dominant tenement (DT) and the servient tenement (ST) must be owned or occupied by different persons.

Accommodates the dominant tenement

This really means that the easement must benefit the land (DT) as such and not the present owner nor activities which the present owner is carrying on.

Hill v *Tupper* (1863) 2 H&C 121 (HC)

Facts

The owner of a canal granted X the exclusive right to put pleasure boats on the canal for profit.

Legal principle

Such a right is just a personal right which did not benefit the land as such and in consequence it was just a licence and did not bind a third party. ▶

> **Analysis**
> This decision reminds us of the boundary in land law between estates and interests in land, which can bind third parties, and personal rights, as here, which do not. However, businesses carried on upon the land may be easements if they are so closely connected with the land that they do benefit it. This seems to be the explanation of *Moody* v *Steggles* (1879).

The question is whether you may need to contrast these cases in an exam.

The DT and the ST must be reasonably adjacent; otherwise there could be no benefit.

Example 8.1

X claims a right of way over land owned by Y but Y's land is two miles away. Although it may benefit X to have the right of way, it can hardly be said to benefit X's land.

Subject of grant

The right claimed must be capable of forming the subject matter of a grant. The basic point is that the right must be sufficiently certain.

Example 8.2

X claims that Y should not build on his land as it would spoil X's view.

A right to a view is not certain enough to be an easement (*Aldred's Case* (1610)). X should have obtained a restrictive covenant over Y's land (check Chapter 7).

Easements should not involve the owner of the ST in positive obligations

See *Regis Property* v *Redman* (1956).

Impress your examiner

There are cases where positive easements have been allowed – e.g. easement of fencing (see *Crow* v *Wood* (1971)). The Law Commission Report (LC 327) recommended (Para. 5.94) that obligations to fence should in future take effect as land obligations.

Recreational easements

Regency Villas Title Ltd v *Diamond Resorts (Europe) Ltd* [2018] UKSC 57

Facts

Owners of villas within an estate which were let as timeshares succeeded in claiming that a transfer to them of rights to use gardens, tennis and squash courts, putting green, croquet lawn, outdoor swimming pool and a golf course on the estate was an easement.

Legal principle

An easement can be for recreational and sporting use and that the question of whether the right accommodates the DT must be considered separately on the facts of every case.

Analysis

Although the leading case of *Re Ellenborough Park* (earlier) upheld an easement of recreation this was only for use of a pleasure ground to, for example, walk over it. Here the Supreme Court developed the law to allow an easement for a much more intensive recreational use and the burden on the servient owners, who had to manage these rights, was correspondingly greater.

No new negative easements?

Phipps v *Pears* [1964] 2 All ER 35 (HC)

Facts

Claim to an easement to protection of one house from rain and frost by another house. This would mean that the other house could not be demolished. The claim was rejected.

Legal principle

The courts are reluctant to allow the creation of new negative easements which would be an undue restriction on an owner's rights over his land.

Analysis

Negative easements give the owner of the dominant land the right to stop the owner of the servient land from using it in a particular way. Although the courts are reluctant to allow the creation of these there is no definite principle that no negative easements can be created. A better way to achieve the aim of many negative easements is to create a restrictive covenant.

Impress your examiner

Note *Coventry (t/a RDC Promotions)* v *Lawrence* (2014) where the SC was prepared to accept the possibility of an easement of noise (in this case from a speedtrack) although here the claim failed on the facts.

An easement cannot subsequently be used for a different purpose

This covers intensification of use (*Jelbert* v *Davis* (1968)).

Easement cannot amount to exclusive use: ouster principle

A distinction must be drawn between an easement and a lease or a licence. Thus, a grant of exclusive possession of land might give rise to a lease (see Chapter 6) but cannot be an easement.

Copeland v *Greenhalf* [1952] 1 All ER 809 (HC)

Facts

The claimant owned land on which the defendant had stored and repaired vehicles for 50 years. He claimed an easement by prescription.

Legal principle

This was a claim to beneficial use of the land and so could not be an easement. Upjohn J described it as: 'virtually a claim to possession of the servient tenement'.

Analysis

If there is what amounts to exclusive use of the land then this looks like a claim to exclusive possession which would be claim to a lease and not an easement. In fact, the ouster principle has been difficult to apply consistently: see easements of car parking and the recommendations of the Law Commission (next). Note also *Wright* v *McAdam* (1949) (later in this chapter).

Impress your examiner

Note the discussion of the ouster principle in connection with easements of car parking that follows. In the Regency Villas case (earlier) the SC felt that ouster was an essentially factual question.

Car parking

This is a likely area for an exam question because:

- Whether there can be an easement of the right to park a car has not been definitively settled although there have been many cases – see, e.g., *Batchelor* v *Marlow* (2001). Note that *Moncrieff* v *Jamieson* (2007) dealt with Scottish law.

- If there is an easement, how does the ouster principle (discussed earlier) affect it? Suppose that X claims the right to park her car on a defined space on land owned by Y. In *Moncrieff* v *Jamieson* Lord Scott in the HL proposed the test of whether the servient owner 'retains possession and, subject to the reasonable exercise of the right in question, control of the servient land'.

The Law Commission Report (LC 327 Paras 3.199–3.208) recommended that the ouster principle should be abolished and that: 'An easement that stops short of exclusive possession, even if it deprives the owner of much of the use of his land, or indeed all reasonable use of it, is valid' (Para. 3.208). This would reverse *Batchelor* v *Marlow*. You should consider if in practice it would be possible to distinguish cases of exclusive possession (not an easement) from where the exercise of the easement deprived the owner of all reasonable use of his land.

One could now argue that the courts are starting to recognise car parking rights on the lines of this Law Commission formula: see, for example, *De Le Cuona v Big Apple Marketing Ltd* [2017] where a right to park in two spaces in a car park was an easement as the owner of the servient land could still could walk across the spaces or back a car into them when coming out of another space when no car was parked in the relevant spaces.

Exam tip

The issue in *De Le Cuona* was between an easement and a lease. Boost your marks in the exam by considering both possibilities where this is relevant.

Impress your examiner

In a general question on the creation or nature of easements, also mention some examples of statutes:

- Access to Neighbouring Land Act 1992.
- Party Wall Act 1996.

Rights of way on public footpaths and bridleways are statutory and are governed by different rules for private easements, with which we are concerned.

Easements, profits and third parties

The rules were set out in Chapter 2 and you should refer to this now to check your knowledge.

Summary

Registered land

- Legal easements and profits created expressly (i.e. by deed) are registrable dispositions.
- Express legal easements and profits, and equitable easements, which were overriding before 13 October 2003, remain overriding.
- New equitable easements and profits must now be entered on the register.
- The only new legal easements and profits that can be overriding are those created:
  - (a) by implied reservation;
  - (b) by implied grant (rule in *Wheeldon* v *Burrows* or s. 62(1), LPA 1925);
  - (c) by prescription (Sch. 3, Para. 3, LRA 2002).

Unregistered land

- Legal easements are binding on all third parties.
- Equitable easements must be registered as land charges if created on or after 1 January 1926. Those created before this date will bind purchasers who have notice of them and will bind donees automatically.

For further detail on these rules check Chapter 2.

Creation of easements

Expressly

- Legal – deed.
- Equitable – written agreement.

In *Chaudhary* v *Yavuz* (2011) the Court of Appeal considered if an equitable easement could give rise to an overriding interest (see Chapter 2).

You should check Chapter 1 and revise the rules on the creation of legal interests in land by deed and equitable interests by written agreement.

Implied reservation in a conveyance

- Necessity, e.g., access to land-locked land. A good case is *Adealon International Corp. Proprietary Ltd* v *Merton LBC* (2007).
- Common intention. See *Wong* v *Beaumont Property Trust Ltd* (1965).

Estoppel

Check Chapter 5 for estoppel. A good case on estoppel easements for the exam is *Ives Investments Ltd* v *High* (1967).

Acquisition of implied easements under the rule in *Wheeldon* v *Burrows*

Wheeldon v *Burrows* (1879) 12 Ch D 31 (HC)

To summarise the facts of this case would add little to an understanding of the legal principle outlined.

Legal principle

On a grant of land, the grantee (e.g. the buyer) will acquire, by implication, all existing easements which:

- are continuous and apparent;
- have been and are at the time of the grant used by the grantor for the benefit of the land – see Alford v Hannaford (2011).

Strictly these are quasi-easements as they are enjoyed by the grantor over her own land.

Analysis

The rule rests on the principle that the grantor cannot derogate (take away from) his own grant, i.e. if land has quasi-easements exercised by one part over another part then these will continue when part of the land with the benefit of the quasi-easements is sold.

Don't be tempted to . . .

Make sure that you are clear about when a situation can involve *Wheeldon* v *Burrows*. A useful guide is to look for a plot of land which is originally in the ownership of one person and is then subdivided.

Exam tip

Wheeldon v *Burrows* easements operate in favour of the buyer and against the seller.

This is how a *Wheeldon* v *Burrows* situation works:

The rule in *Wheeldon* v *Burrows* allows Y to claim as an implied easement a right of way over the land retained by X.

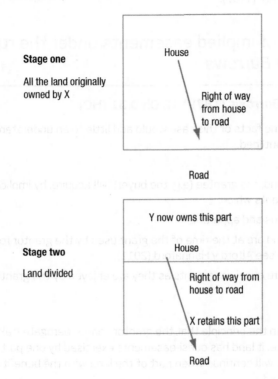

Stage one

All the land originally owned by X

House

Right of way from house to road

Road

Stage two

Land divided

Y now owns this part

House

Right of way from house to road

X retains this part

Road

The rule in *Wheeldon* v *Burrows* also applies where X in the diagram example sells all the land and grants part of the land to one person (Y) in our example, and grants the other part to Z (i.e. the part retained by X in our example). Therefore, X no longer retains any land and so it will be Z who is bound by Y's implied easement.

Are easements created by the rule in *Wheeldon* v *Burrows* legal or equitable?

This depends on the document which transferred the land (e.g. the document under which X transferred to Y).

If it was a deed (which it would be here), the easement will be legal, but if it was simply by an enforceable written agreement, it will be equitable.

The Law Commission Report (LC 327) recommended that the methods of creation of easements by necessity, common intention and under *Wheeldon* v *Burrows* should be abolished and replaced by a single statutory principle that easements will be implied where they are necessary for the reasonable use of the land (Para. 3.45) bearing in mind five factors, e.g., the potential interference caused to the servient land by the use of the easement or inconvenience to the servient owner. Profits could not be created in this way.

Acquisition of implied easements under section 62(1) of the LPA 1925

Section 62(1), Law of Property Act 1925

A conveyance of the land shall be deemed to convey and shall operate to convey with the land all privileges, easements, rights appertaining or reputed to appertain to the land at the time of the conveyance.

This provision is not controversial in itself: it merely provides that on a conveyance of land certain rights that it has (e.g. easements and profits) are automatically also conveyed. What is controversial is the use which has been made of it to create easements where none seemed to exist before.

Wright v McAdam [1949] 2 All ER 556 (CA)

Facts
The defendant let a flat to the claimant and gave her permission (i.e. a licence) to store coal in it. He later granted her a new tenancy.

Legal principle
The grant of the tenancy was a conveyance under section 62(1), and as a right to store coal was a right capable of being granted by law the grant of the new tenancy had the effect of converting what was a licence into an easement.

Analysis
This decision was controversial as it enabled a licence (not a property right) to be elevated into an easement (a property right). It also appeared that this was an exclusive right of storage and so the court should not have held that it was an easement under the ouster principle.

Exam tip

- -

Check that the right is capable of being an easement. In fact in *Wright* v *McAdam* the right of storage appeared to be exclusive, which might not have qualified it for an easement. (See the earlier discussion of the ouster principle.)

- -

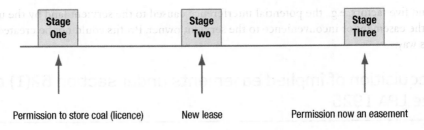

Stage One	Stage Two	Stage Three
Permission to store coal (licence)	New lease	Permission now an easement

The traditional view was that there were two requirements for section 62(1) to apply:

(a) There is diversity of occupation, i.e. each piece of land is occupied by different people (*Sovmots Investments Ltd* v *Environment Secretary* (1977)).

(b) The easement is continuous and apparent.

However, in *P & S Platt Ltd* v *Crouch* (2003) it was held that provided the easement was continuous and apparent, there was no need for diversity of occupation and this was approved by the Court of Appeal in *Alford* v *Hannaford* (2011). This case is an excellent example of the relationship between *Wheeldon* v *Burrows* and section 62 of the LPA 1925.

Don't be tempted to . . .

Do not just apply section 62 where the land was previously occupied by the same person; ask as well if the existence of the easement was continuous and apparent. The facts of *Platt* were unusual as they concerned two distinct pieces of land owned by the seller; a hotel and an adjacent island with mooring rights used by hotel guests. The hotel was sold and the buyer successfully claimed that the sale transferred the mooring rights also as these were continuous and apparent. Most sales (e.g. of a house) will just involve one piece of land and so any rights exercised by the seller over parts of it will not be apparent. If this is so then the only possibility of acquiring an easement will be through *Wheeldon* v *Burrows*. See the answer guidelines at the end of this chapter for an illustration.

The Law Commission Report (LC 327) recommended (Para. 3.64) that the principle in *Wright* v *McAdam* should be abolished and that section 62 of the LPA shall no longer operate to transform what it calls 'precarious benefits' (i.e. licences) into easements. Section 62 itself should remain but only apply to easements and not to profits (Para. 3.68). See also Douglas (2015).

Prescription

Rights acquired by **prescription** are legal as they are presumed to have been granted by deed. Prescription means the acquisition of easements and profits by long use.

Conditions for prescription

Use must be without:

* force;
* secrecy;
* permission.

See *London Tara Hotel Ltd* v *Kensington Close Hotel Ltd* (2011) for a modern example of where use by prescription was not secret nor by permission and so an easement by prescription was established.

Types of prescription

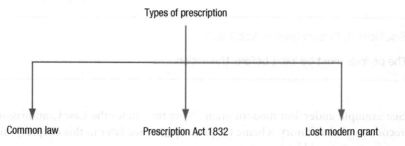

* *Common law* – from 'time immemorial' – 1189 – in practice for as long as anyone can remember and it could have been since 1189.

Exam tip

If the DT is a house, then this method cannot apply as the house will not have existed in 1189.

* Under the Prescription Act 1832.

Section 2, Prescription Act 1832

Claim to an easement by prescription requires 20 years' continuous use, but where the easement was exercised with the oral agreement of the servient owner, it is 40 years.

- A claim by prescription is based on a presumed grant and the claim will fail if the presumed grantor had no capacity to grant the easement. See *Housden v Conservators of Wimbledon and Putney Common* (2008).
- Note the periods for profits: 30 and 60 years.

> ### Section 3, Prescription Act 1832
>
> Claim to an easement of light requires 20 years' continuous use – no provision for an extra 20 years where exercised with the permission of the owner.

- Note: Rights of Light Act 1959: owner of ST can block a right to light by registering a notice. The Law Commission has published Report (356): Rights to Light (2014). Make sure that you are aware of its main points.

> ### Section 4, Prescription Act 1832
>
> The periods must be 'next before' the action.

- See example under 'lost modern grant'. Note that under the Law Commission's recommended statutory scheme for prescription (see later in this chapter) this requirement would be removed.
- Discontinuance for less than a year is ignored.

The relationship between these sections is shown by this example:

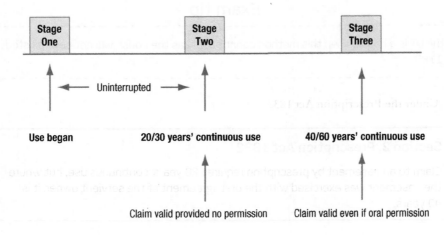

- Where there is written permission for the use of the land, there can be no acquisition of an easement or profit by prescription.
- **Lost modern grant**. In an exam question this should be mentioned as the last possibility.

Lost modern grant

The court assumes two things that have not, in fact, occurred:

- there was a grant of an easement;
- it has been lost.

Example 8.3

This is based on a profit.

X has allowed his sheep to graze on Y's land for many years but did not do so for the last 18 months because they were diseased.

- No claim to a profit at common law: cannot prove use since 1189.
- Prescription Act does not apply as discontinuance more than a year – section 4 applies – no period of prescription as period not next before action.
- So, have to rely on lost modern grant.

See *Tehidy Minerals* v *Norman* (1971) for a case example.

The Law Commission Report (LC 327) recommends (Para. 3.123) that all the discussed means of acquiring an easement or profit by prescription should be abolished and:

- profits cannot be acquired by prescription;
- easements can be acquired by 20 years' continuous use provided that:

  (a) it was use without force, stealth or permission;

  (b) it was not use contrary to the criminal law.

Profits

Exam tip

Check carefully what the right is: an easement or a profit?

Note the following rules on profits and how they differ from those on easements:

- No requirement of a dominant tenement.
- The rule in *Wheeldon* v *Burrows* does not apply to the creation of profits but section 62(1), LPA 1925 does.

▶

- The periods of prescription are longer: see earlier.
- Apart from this, the rules are generally the same.
- Note how the Law Commission's proposals affect profits: a profit could only be created by express grant, reservation or by statute and not by implication or by prescription (Para. 3.9).

Law Commission proposals for reform

In addition to the proposals mentioned earlier, the Law Commission in its report (LC 327) published in June 2011, proposed that section 84(1) of the LPA 1925 (see Chapter 7) should also allow the discharge or modification of easements or profits but only provided that the modified interest shall not be less convenient to the benefited owner and not more burdensome to the land affected (Para. 7.60). The Queen's Speech setting out the Government's legislative proposals for the 2016–17 session promised a Law of Property Bill to give effect to these recommendations, but at the time of writing (October 2019) there has been no news of this Bill.

Putting it all together

Sample question

Could you answer this question? What follows is a typical essay question that could arise on this topic. Additionally, a sample problem question and guidance on tackling it can be found on the companion website.

Essay question

Many easements are implied rather than created by express grant. Critically analyse the methods by which easements can be created by implication.

Answer guidelines

Approaching the question

This question asks for not only an explanation of the methods by which easements are acquired by implication but also a critical analysis. Keep this in mind!

Important points to include

Explain what acquisition by implication means and how it contrasts with express acquisition.

Move on to the main methods of acquisition by implication – see earlier – and make sure that, in particular, you explain creation by *Wheeldon* v *Burrows* and section 62(1) of the LPA 1925 clearly.

Emphasise recent cases in this area and demonstrate a clear knowledge of how the decision in the *Platt* case *may* have expanded the scope of section 62 on acquisition of easements at the expense of *Wheeldon* v *Burrows*.

A possible conclusion would be that the present law is complex and confusing and to ask whether there is any need for implied creation of easements.

You should then end by looking at the ideas in the Law Commission Report.

Impress your examiner

Consider the practical problems for a purchaser created by implied easements and look at the report of *Moncrieff* v *Jamieson*, which was also a case of implied creation of an easement (of parking) attached to an express grant of a right of way. Discuss the potential problems to which this decision gives rise as explained in the article by Junior (2008) (see the 'Key further reading' section).

You could also question whether section 62(1) does create new easements by implication or expressly, i.e. by the express word of the statute.

Key case summary

Key case	How to use	Related topics
Hill v *Tupper*	To explain that an easement must accommodate the dominant tenement.	Characteristics of easements.
Regency Villas Title Ltd v *Diamond Resorts (Europe) Ltd*	To show that there can be an easement of recreational rights.	Characteristics of easements.
Phipps v *Pears*	To illustrate the point that the courts are reluctant to allow the creation of new categories of negative easements.	Negative easements.

Key case	How to use	Related topics
Copeland v *Greenhalf*	To explain that a claim to exclusive use of the land cannot amount to an easement.	Easements contrasted with leases.
Wheeldon v *Burrows*	To show how an easement by implication can be created on a sale of part of the land where the seller retains the other part.	Implied easements. Law Commission proposals.
Wright v *McAdam*	To show how an easement by implication can be created by use of section 62 of the LPA 1925.	Implied easements. Law Commission proposals.

Key further reading

Key articles/reports	How to use	Related topics
Bevan, C. (2019) Opening Pandora's box? Recreation pure and simple: easements in the Supreme Court. 1 *Conv.* 55.	This is a detailed analysis of the decision in the *Regency Villas* case which also looks at its potential impact on the law of easements.	Easements.
Mc Leod, G. (2019) The traditional concept hits the bunker: easements after *Regency Villas Title Ltd* v *Diamond Resorts (Europe) Ltd.* 3 *Conv.* 250.	This questions the argument, implicit in the *Regency Villas* case, that, in principle, it should be property law which secures the protection of new and/or extensive uses of another's land.	Easements.

Key articles/reports	How to use	Related topics
Douglas, S. (2015) How to reform section 62 of the Law of Property Act 1925. 1 *Conv*. 13.	Douglas would go further than the recommendations of the Law Commission (2011) and repeal section 62 altogether. He argues that it is superfluous because on a land transfer all rights 'appertaining or appurtenant' to land, e.g. easements, are transferred automatically with the land anyway.	Creation of implied easements under s.62 of the LPA 1925.
Junior, G. (2008) Warning – parking problems ahead (*Moncrieff* v *Jamieson* applied). 1 *SLT* 1.	*Moncrieff* v *Jamieson* is now the leading case on easements of parking so this article is a must-read.	Easements of parking.
Law Commission (2011) Report 327, Making land work: easements, covenants and profits *à prendre*.	This is essential reading for all students of easements and profits. Not only does it contain proposals for reform of the law, which are likely to be implemented at some future date, but it also contains a lucid account of the present law.	Easements and profits.
This report is considered by Sutton (2013) On the brink of land obligations again. 1 *Conv*. 17–29.	Read the article by Sutton alongside the Law Commission's Report for a valuable critique.	
Law Commission Report (356): Rights to light (2014).	This is an important and often misunderstood area and reading this report will clarify it for you.	Rights of light.

go.pearson.com/uk/lawexpress

Go online to access more revision support including quizzes to test your knowledge, sample questions with answer guidelines, printable versions of the topic maps, and more!

9

Mortgages

Revision checklist

Essential points you should know:

- Mortgages as proprietary interests in land and as contracts
- When a mortgage is legal and when a mortgage is equitable
- Principles on which the courts will intervene to set a mortgage aside
- When a mortgage may be affected by undue influence
- Remedies of the mortgagee and principles applicable to each

Topic map

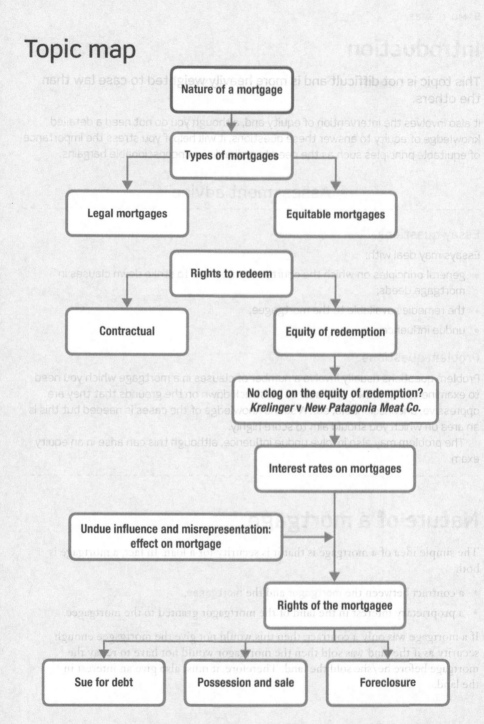

Nature of a mortgage

Types of mortgages

Legal mortgages

Equitable mortgages

Rights to redeem

Contractual

Equity of redemption

No clog on the equity of redemption?
Krelinger v *New Patagonia Meat Co.*

Interest rates on mortgages

Undue influence and misrepresentation: effect on mortgage

Rights of the mortgagee

Sue for debt

Possession and sale

Foreclosure

A printable version of this topic map is available from **go.pearson.com/uk/lawexpress**

Introduction

This topic is not difficult and is more heavily weighted to case law than the others.

It also involves the intervention of equity and, although you do not need a detailed knowledge of equity to answer these questions, it will help if you stress the importance of equitable principles such as the need to strike down unconscionable bargains.

Assessment advice

- -

Essay questions

Essays may deal with:

- general principles on which the courts can intervene to strike down clauses in mortgage deeds;
- the remedies available to the mortgagee;
- undue influence.

Problem questions

Problem questions usually involve a number of clauses in a mortgage which you need to examine to see if they are liable to be struck down on the grounds that they are oppressive, unconscionable, etc. A sound knowledge of the cases is needed but this is an area on which you should aim to score highly.

The problem may also involve undue influence, although this can arise in an equity exam.

- -

Nature of a mortgage

The simple idea of a mortgage is that it is security for a loan. In fact, a mortgage is both:

- a contract between the **mortgagor** and the **mortgagee**;
- a proprietary interest in the land of the mortgagor granted to the mortgagee.

If a mortgage was only a contract, then this would not give the mortgagee enough security as if the land was sold then the mortgagor would not have to repay the mortgage before he/she sold the land. Therefore, it must also give an interest in the land.

To be clear: the borrower in a mortgage is the *mortgagor*, the lender in a mortgage is the *mortgagee*.

Types of mortgages

A mortgage of land is normally a charge by deed by way of legal mortgage.

This will be legal but an equitable mortgage can be created by an agreement which complies with section 2 of the Law of Property (Miscellaneous Provisions) Act 1989. Check in Chapter 1 that you can recall these provisions.

Note that a mortgage by deed which is not registered will be equitable also.

Rights to redeem

Redemption of the mortgage means simply paying it off so that the land is free from the mortgage.

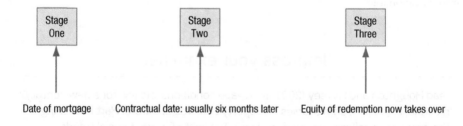

Stage One	Stage Two	Stage Three
Date of mortgage	Contractual date: usually six months later	Equity of redemption now takes over

Impress your examiner

Equity played a major part in developing the law on mortgages and this is for historical reasons.

Mortgages were traditionally entered into when someone needed a loan as they were in debt and, as they might be persuaded into a mortgage on terms that were very onerous, equity aimed to protect them. Today mortgages are usually made because a person wishes to buy or lease a house. However, equity still insists on the equity of redemption, and it claims the right to set a mortgage aside (see later in this chapter).

Don't be tempted to . . .

Be sure that you understand exactly when the courts can intervene to set aside the terms of a mortgage. This can arise:

- in an essay;
- in a problem question, where you can gain extra marks by not just quoting cases which deal with the particular point but also stressing that in the background there is a debate on the precise extent to which the courts can intervene.

Note Greene MR in the *Knightsbridge* case (1939) (see under 'Equity of redemption'): 'But equity does not reform commercial transactions because they are unreasonable. It is concerned to see two things – one that the essential requirements of a mortgage transaction are observed, and the other that oppressive or unconscionable terms are not enforced.'

Note the distinction drawn by Greene MR between 'unreasonable' and 'oppressive or unconscionable'.

Impress your examiner

Read Houghton and Livesey (2001) Mortgage conditions: old law for a new century? In Cooke, E. (ed.). *Modern Studies in Property Law,* Vol. 1. Oxford: Hart Publishing. This gives an excellent survey of the law in the light of current social trends.

Equity of redemption

A fundamental principle is that the mortgagor must be able to redeem early. However, as this is equity this is not an absolute rule:

Knightsbridge Estates Trust Ltd v Byrne [1939] Ch 441 (HC)

Facts
A commercial mortgage at ordinary interest rates where there was no inequality of bargaining power provided that it could not be redeemed for 40 years. The borrower was not allowed to repay earlier.

Legal principle

There is no absolute rule that a mortgage cannot prevent early redemption.

Analysis

The parties had entered into the agreement freely and the bargain was not oppressive. Thus there was no reason for equity to intervene. Equity does not set aside bargains just because they are unwise.

Fairclough v Swan Brewery [1912] AC 565 (PC)

Facts

The mortgagor was an assignee of a lease which had seventeen and a half years to run. The final mortgage instalment was due only six weeks before the lease expired.

Legal principle

Where the redemption date of the mortgage on a lease is at the point when the lease is about to expire, then redemption is of no value to the mortgagor. Therefore, the mortgagor was entitled to redeem earlier.

Analysis

The point was that the right to redeem was illusory and so early redemption was allowed. However, there was no evidence of oppression and the decision conflicts with the earlier one of *Santley v Wilde* (1899). It is possible that *Fairclough* may be reconsidered in future.

No clog on the equity of redemption?

This means that on redemption all mortgage obligations must be discharged but, in fact, the courts have not always applied this rule rigidly.

Krelinger v New Patagonia Meat and Cold Storage Co. Ltd [1914] AC 25 (HL)

Facts

A firm of woolbrokers lent money on a mortgage which could be repaid at any time in the next five years. The mortgagor also agreed to give the mortgagee first refusal on all their sheepskins and to pay commission on any sold to a third party. This agreement was to last for the full five years. This collateral agreement was upheld. ▶

> **Legal principle**
> A collateral advantage for the mortgagee may be upheld where it does not prevent the mortgagor getting his land back in the same form as when it was mortgaged.
>
> **Analysis**
> The principle is that if the collateral advantage for the mortgagee is not a fetter on the right to redeem but a collateral bargain then it will be upheld. In fact, this case together with others on the equity of redemption show the essential fluidity of the law in this area as we are applying equitable principles.

Equity also regards a term of the mortgage that gives the mortgagee an option to purchase as a clog on the equity of redemption. See *Samuel* v *Jarrah Timber* (1904).

Impress your examiner

Consider that the House of Lords came to this conclusion in *Samuel* v *Jarrah Timber* with reluctance, and it may reconsider this rule in future. Compare *Reeve* v *Lisle* (1902) where the term was in a separate agreement and was upheld. In *Warnborough* v *Garmite Ltd* (2003) it was held that the rule in *Samuel* v *Jarrah* would not apply where the mortgage was part of a more complex transaction. Here the mortgage was part of a sale and purchase agreement.

Another instance of a clog on the equity of redemption is provided by *Noakes* v *Rice* (1902).

Interest rates on mortgages

These are subject to the general principle that equity will set aside a bargain which is oppressive and unconscionable.

Look at *Cityland and Property (Holdings) Ltd* v *Dabrah* (1968) and *Multiservice Bookbinding* v *Marden* (1978) and note the different approaches in each.

> **Sections 140A and 140B, Consumer Credit Act 1974 (inserted by ss. 19 and 20, Consumer Credit Act 2006)**
>
> The courts have wide powers over a credit agreement (including a mortgage agreement) where it is unfair to the debtor (i.e. the mortgagor) because of any of its terms, the way in which it is exercised, or any other thing done by the creditor (i.e. the mortgagee).

Exam tip

- -

Check if the lender is an individual or a company. If the latter, then this Act will not apply.

- -

Exam tip

- -

Section 140 replaces the previous sections 137–140 of the Consumer Credit Act 1974.

- -

Undue influence and mortgages

Undue influence is an equitable doctrine that is difficult to define precisely but, in essence, it aims to prevent the vulnerable from exploitation. It is really directed at the manner in which a transaction is entered into.

You should check if it is likely to be examined in land law, as it can also arise in an equity exam, but it is certainly relevant to mortgages.

Royal Bank of Scotland plc v Etridge (No. 2) [2001] 4 All ER 449 (HL)

Facts
The facts of this case would add little to an understanding of the legal principle which follows. Remember that examiners are usually looking for an understanding of the legal principle and that just reciting the facts in an exam will not improve your grade.

Legal principle
Lord Nicholls held that there is a distinction between:

(a) cases of actual coercion;

(b) cases where the undue influence arises from a particular relationship.

In (b) there is a subdivision between:

(i) cases where there is a relationship of trust and confidence. If it is established that there has been a transaction which calls for some explanation, then the burden shifts to the person seeking to uphold the transaction to show that there was no undue influence;

(ii) certain types of relationship where one party has acquired influence over another who is vulnerable and dependent and by whom substantial gifts are ▶

---

not normally to be expected, e.g. parent and child, trustee and beneficiary, and medical adviser and patient. In these cases there is a presumption of undue influence by the stronger party over the weaker.

Analysis

This is now the leading authority on what constitutes undue influence. It can be a troublesome doctrine to pin down and the categories just listed are especially helpful. If you need a straightforward example of undue influence to fix the doctrine in your mind see *Re Craig* (1971).

Exam tip

The most likely area of undue influence for an exam question is (b)(i) in the list just provided. It should be noted that (b)(ii) does not include husband and wife, a common scenario for exam problems and so this situation would fall into (b)(i).

Don't be tempted to . . .

Remember to deal with the presumption of undue influence in a question on mortgages. Having first decided that you are dealing with a possible undue influence case, you should move on immediately to see where it falls in the categories listed under *Royal Bank of Scotland plc v Etridge*. This is vital to know if undue influence has to be proved or not.

Undue influence can affect a mortgage in two ways:

(1) Where the mortgagee has exercised undue influence to induce the mortgagor to enter into the mortgage. A possible example is *National Westminster Bank* v *Morgan* (1985).

(2) Where the mortgagee has not exercised undue influence but it is claimed that a third party has and this affects the mortgagee. This is the most likely scenario for the exam.

Undue influence and third parties

This area has become of great importance in recent years especially since the decision of the House of Lords in *Barclays Bank* v *O'Brien* (1994).

Students often jump straight to this issue when they see it in a problem question and do not first ask if there has been undue influence in the first place. Do this first!

Example 9.1

John persuades Claud, his partner, to enter into a second mortgage of their jointly owned home to the Viper Bank in order to secure some business debts of John. It is clear that John exercised undue influence over Claud to persuade him to sign. The question is whether the Viper Bank is affected by what John has done. If it is not, then, although John may be liable to Claud, the actual mortgage is unaffected.

Exam tip

The principles stated by Lord Browne-Wilkinson in *Barclays Bank* v *O'Brien* were the starting point of the law here. However, they have been overtaken by those stated by Lord Nicholls in *Etridge* (next), and in a problem question you should concentrate on applying these.

Note: In the following case the word 'surety' is used and here it means the person who has agreed to guarantee the debt, etc. – Claud in Example 9.1.

Royal Bank of Scotland plc (No. 2) v *Etridge* [2001] 4 All ER 449 (HL)

Facts

The facts of this case would add little to an understanding of the legal principle which follows. Remember that examiners are usually looking for an understanding of the legal principle and that just reciting the facts in an exam will not improve your grade.

Legal principles

These were stated by Lord Nicholls as follows:

(a) A lender is put on inquiry when one person offers to stand surety for the debts of:

- his or her spouse;
- a person involved in a non-commercial relationship with the surety and the lender is aware of this;
- any company in which any of the above hold shares.

(b) Steps to be taken when a lender is put on inquiry:

- The lender must contact the surety and request that they nominate a solicitor.
- The surety must reply nominating a solicitor.

▶

- The lender must, with the consent of the surety, disclose to the solicitor all relevant information – both the debtor's financial position and the details of the proposed loan.
- The solicitor must advise the surety in a face-to-face meeting at which the debtor is not present. The advice must cover an explanation of the documentation and the risks to the surety in signing, and emphasise that the surety must decide whether to proceed.
- The solicitor must, if satisfied that the surety wishes to proceed, send written confirmation to the lender that the solicitor has explained the nature of the documents and their implications for the surety.

Analysis

There had been many cases following *Barclays Bank v O'Brien* which attempted to clarify exactly when a surety can be liable but the law was still unclear until the concise and simple procedures listed here were laid down by Lord Nicholls. These have been applied in subsequent cases.

Impress your examiner

The principle in *O'Brien* and the decision in *Etridge* have been the subject of a great deal of academic debate. A good place to start is the article by Andrews (2002).

Consequences of undue influence

If the mortgage is affected by undue influence, then it is voidable.

Don't be tempted to . . .

Make sure that you deal with the *extent* to which the mortgage will be set aside. *TSB Bank plc v Camfield* (1995): the whole mortgage was set aside. *Dunbar Bank plc v Nadeem* (1997): it was only set aside on condition that the claimant accounted to the mortgagee for the benefit she had from it.

Misrepresentation and mortgages

Instead of or in addition to the possibility of undue influence, an exam question may ask you if there has been **misrepresentation**. You will probably not need to remember much on this from your contract days, just the definition: misrepresentation here means an untrue statement of fact which induces a person to enter into a transaction.

Look out for where undue influence and misrepresentation are possibly combined, i.e. X uses undue influence to persuade Y, his partner, to sign a mortgage but also lies about how much the mortgage is for.

Rights of the mortgagee

To sue for debt

- A contractual right and allows the mortgagee to recover the debt.

Possession and sale

Possession

- Allows the mortgagee to take possession (the mortgage deed allows this at any time during the mortgage) and to sell the property. Any surplus belongs to the mortgagor.

Section 36, Administration of Justice Act (AJA) 1970

This applies to mortgages of dwelling houses where the mortgagee seeks possession. It allows the court, if it appears that the mortgagor will, within a reasonable period, be able to pay sums due under the mortgage, or remedy a default consisting of a breach arising under it, to:

- adjourn the proceedings; or
- on giving an order for possession, to stay or suspend execution of it or postpone the date for delivery of possession.

Section 36 applies to both legal and equitable mortgages.

See *Cheltenham & Gloucester BSc v Norgan* (1996) for the principles on which this should be exercised. An illustration of how section 36 works, useful for exam purposes, is *Preferred Mortgages Ltd v McCombe* [2015].

Impress your examiner

Consider the relationship between section 36 and the mortgagee's right to possession. In *Ropaigealach v Barclays Bank plc* (2000) it was held that where the mortgagee takes possession relying on its common law power to do so without ▶

a court order (see above) then the court cannot exercise its powers under section 36. Note too *Horsham Properties* v *Clark* (later in this section) for another instance of where the protections for mortgagors in section 36 were avoided by the mortgagee. See Whitehouse (2019) on the relationship between section 36 and the wider provisions of the Consumer Credit Act 1974 (outlined earlier in this chapter).

Sale

An exam question may ask you if a mortgagee can apply to sell the mortgaged property. The mortgage deed normally includes a power of sale but, if not, a power of sale is implied into every mortgage by section 101 of the LPA 1925.

Section 101(1) and (4), Law of Property Act 1925

Section 101(1): the mortgagee's statutory power of sale arises when:

- the mortgage was by deed;
- the mortgage money has become due (i.e. the redemption date has passed) or an instalment of the mortgage repayments is due.

Section 101(4) provides that for these conditions to apply the mortgage must contain no expression of a contrary intention.

If the conditions in section 101 are met, you then need to ask if the power of sale is actually exercisable, and here we turn to section 103.

Section 103, Law of Property Act 1925

A power of sale is exercisable if any one of these conditions are met:

- A notice requiring payment of the mortgage money due has been served and the mortgagor has been in default for three months following this.
- Interest under the mortgage has remained unpaid for two months after becoming due.
- There has been a breach of some mortgage term other than one for the payment of money or interest.

When selling, the mortgagee can have regard to his own interests and does not sell as trustee for the mortgagor (*Cuckmere Brick Co. Ltd* v *Mutual Finance* (1971)).

Any surplus on the sale after all liabilities, costs and expenses have been met belongs to the mortgagor but, as the mortgagee, when selling, does not have to consider the mortgagor's interests, any surplus may be small as the mortgagee may not sell for the best price.

Foreclosure

- Rarely granted – vests the property in the mortgagee and the mortgagor has no rights to any surplus. As this remedy is widely felt to be archaic the question is whether it should be abolished.

Appointment of a receiver

This is the right to appoint a receiver to manage and administer the mortgaged property. As with the power of sale, this is generally included in the mortgage deed but, if not, it is implied by section 101 of the LPA.

Horsham Properties Group Ltd v Clark [2008] EWHC 2327

Facts

The mortgagee acting under a power contained in section 101(1)(iii) of the LPA 1925 (see earlier box and discussion) and their own mortgage conditions, appointed receivers of the mortgaged property after the mortgagors fell into arrears. The purchasers, who had bought it from the receivers, then claimed possession as against the mortgagors who had effectively become trespassers in their own home. The purchasers were entitled to possession as of right and section 36 of the AJA (see earlier box and discussion) did not help the mortgagors as it only applied where mortgagees sought possession. The mortgagors claimed that this violated their right to the peaceful enjoyment of their possessions guaranteed by Article 1 of the First Protocol to the European Convention on Human Rights, as incorporated into UK law by the Human Rights Act 1998.

Legal principle

The mortgagee had proceeded under the contract by using its mortgage conditions and so the ECHR was not engaged. Even if it had, the power of the mortgagee to sell the mortgaged property was a 'central and essential aspect of the security'.

▶

> **Analysis**
> This decision was felt to be unsatisfactory and a private members' Bill, the Home Repossession (Protection) Bill, was introduced. This would have amended section 101 of the LPA 1925 by ensuring that a mortgagee of a dwelling house could not exercise the power of sale without first obtaining an order of the court, and the court would be given substantially the same powers as those found currently in section 36 of the AJA 1970. However, it did not become law.

Exam tip

A reference to the ECHR and its application to actions for possession of land will earn you extra marks in an answer on the remedies of the mortgagee. (Look at the discussion in Chapter 1.) See Greer (2009) on this case and Loveland (2014) on later litigation.

Putting it all together

Sample question

Could you answer this question? What follows is a typical essay question that could arise on this topic. Additionally, a sample problem question and guidance on tackling it are included on the companion website.

Essay question

'If the freedom of home-owners to make economic use of their homes is not to be frustrated, a bank must be able to have confidence that a wife's signature of the necessary guarantee and charge will be binding on her.' Lord Nicholls in *Royal Bank of Scotland plc (No. 2)* v *Etridge* (2001).

To what extent do you consider that the present law on this area does enable banks to have this necessary confidence?

Answer guidelines

Approaching the question

This question does not require a general description of the law on third parties and undue influence but a carefully structured discussion of the actual issue. The example given in this chapter of third parties and undue influence would make a good start.

Important points to include

Explain what undue influence and misrepresentation is.

- Mention *Barclays Bank* v *O'Brien* and how it began the development of this part of the law.
- Explain *Etridge* and discuss whether the balance between the interests of banks, lenders and sureties is maintained by the principles in *Etridge*.

Impress your examiner

Refer to Lord Nicholls's speech in *Etridge* and refer to the views of academic authors – see the 'Key further reading' section.

Key case summary

Key case	How to use	Related topics
Knightsbridge Estates Trust Ltd v *Byrne*	To explain that there is no absolute rule that a mortgage deed can never prevent early redemption.	Equity of redemption.
Fairclough v *Swan Brewery*	To explain that where the redemption date of the mortgage on a lease is at the point when the lease is about to expire, then redemption is of no value to the mortgagor.	Mortgage of a lease.
Krelinger v *New Patagonia Meat and Cold Storage Co. Ltd*	To show that there are circumstances where a collateral advantage in a mortgage can continue after the mortgage has been redeemed.	Clog on the equity of redemption.
Royal Bank of Scotland plc v *Etridge (No. 2)*	To explain when the doctrine of undue influence may apply so as to set aside a transaction.	Undue influence and mortgages.

▶

Key case	How to use	Related topics
Royal Bank of Scotland plc v *Etridge (No. 2)*	To state the steps which a lender should take to avoid being affected by the undue influence of another, e.g. the borrower.	Setting aside of transactions affected by undue influence.
Horsham Properties Group Ltd v *Clark*	To contrast appointment of a receiver by a mortgagee with proceedings under section 36 of the AJA 1970.	Remedies of the mortgagee.

Key further reading

Key articles/reports	How to use	Related topics
Andrews, G. (2002) Undue influence – where's the disadvantage? 66 *Conv.* 456.	This is an excellent analysis of the important decision in *Royal Bank of Scotland* v *Etridge*	Undue influence. Mortgages. Equitable doctrines.
Greer, S. (2009) *Horsham Properties Group Ltd* v *Clark*: possession – mortgagee's right or discretionary remedy? 6 *Conv.* 516.	This analyses the controversial case of *Horsham Properties* and suggests changes to the law. It is useful to read this article with that by Loveland (next).	Remedies of the mortgagee.
Loveland, I. (2014) Peaceable entry to mortgaged premises: considering the doctrine's compatibility with the HRA 1998. 5 *Conv.* 381.	This asks if the common law doctrine of peaceable entry by the mortgagee is compatible with the right to respect for one's home under Art. 8 of the European Convention on Human Rights 1950, and if *Ropaigealach* v *Barclays Bank Plc* remains good law.	Remedies of the mortgagee.

Key articles/reports	How to use	Related topics
Whitehouse, L. (2019) Mortgage Possession at a crossroads: which way should we turn? 3. *Conv.* 227.	This argues that in mortgage possession cases more use should be made of the Consumer Credit Act (CCA) 1974, than s.36 of the AJA 1970 as the CCA gives more protection to mortgagors.	Remedies of the mortgagee.

go.pearson.com/uk/lawexpress

Go online to access more revision support including quizzes to test your knowledge, sample questions with answer guidelines, printable versions of the topic maps, and more!

10

Adverse possession

Revision checklist

Essential points you should know:

- Meaning of factual possession and intention to possess
- Relevance of an acknowledgement of the owner's title
- Significance of the land being earmarked
- Mechanics of acquiring title: unregistered land and registered land
- Impact of the Human Rights Act

Topic map

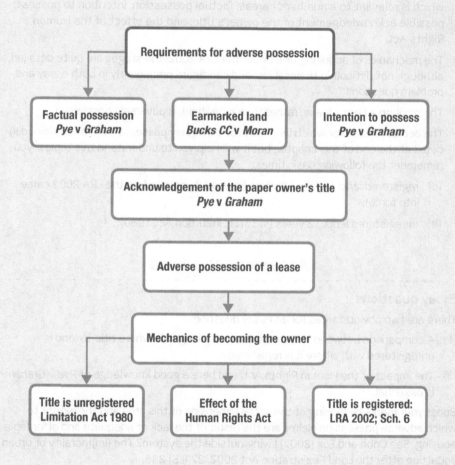

Requirements for adverse possession

Factual possession
Pye v *Graham*

Earmarked land
Bucks CC v *Moran*

Intention to possess
Pye v *Graham*

Acknowledgement of the paper owner's title
Pye v *Graham*

Adverse possession of a lease

Mechanics of becoming the owner

Title is unregistered
Limitation Act 1980

Effect of the
Human Rights Act

Title is registered:
LRA 2002; Sch. 6

A printable version of this topic map is available from **go.pearson.com/uk/lawexpress**

Introduction

The key to this topic is to go through all the stages in how title is acquired by adverse possession logically, paying particular attention to:

- The effect of the decision in *Pye* v *Graham* (2002) – this is a really vital case which is relevant to a number of areas: factual possession; intention to possess; possible acknowledgement of the owner's title; and the effect of the Human Rights Act.
- The mechanics of acquiring title under the LRA 2002: the stages are quite detailed, although not difficult in themselves, and can figure prominently in both essay and problem questions.
- The position where a lease, rather than a freehold, is adversely possessed.
- The actual periods for which land must be adversely possessed will be explained in detail at the end of this chapter, but it will help you to understand this topic if you remember the following basic times:
  - (a) *registered land*: initially 10 years (it was 12 years before the LRA 2002 came into force);
  - (b) *unregistered land*: 12 years (s. 15(1) Limitation Act 1980).

Assessment advice

Essay questions

There are two obvious areas for an essay question:

(1) A comparison between the methods of acquiring title where title to land is unregistered with where it is registered.

(2) The impact of the Human Rights Act, and here a good knowledge of *Pye* v *Graham* is essential.

Boost your marks by looking at the social dimension of this area and the extent to which adverse possession claims are the result of the lack of adequate and affordable housing. See Cobb and Fox (2007) Living outside the system? The (im)morality of urban squatting after the Land Registration Act 2002. 27 (LS) 236.

Problem questions

A problem question will almost certainly involve most of the areas in this chapter: the extent to which the land has been adversely possessed; the possible effect of an acknowledgement of the owner's title (marks to be gained here by appreciating that the law is not entirely clear); earmarking of the land for future use; and the actual application for registration.

Do not start your answer until you have checked:

- Dates: make a note of when possession began and the date now.
- Is it a claim to a freehold or to a leasehold?
- Is title to the land registered or unregistered? As always in land law, do check whether it is an alternative in the question on the basis that title is registered or unregistered.

- -

Factual possession

This is often referred to as the '*corpus possessionis*'.

These words of Slade J in *Powell* v *McFarlane* (1977) were accepted by the HL in *Pye* v *Graham* as representing the law: 'Factual possession signifies an appropriate degree of physical control . . . Everything must depend on the particular circumstances but broadly, I think what must be shown . . . is that the alleged possessor has been dealing with the land as an occupying owner might have been expected to deal with it and that no one else has done so.'

Pye (J.A.) Oxford Ltd v Graham [2002] 3 All ER 865 (HL)

Facts
The defendants farmed land where they grazed cattle, maintained the boundary, trimmed the hedges and re-seeded the land. The paper owner had no key to the gate to the land.

Legal principle
Sufficient factual possession.

Analysis
This is a straightforward illustration of a case of factual possession. A recent illustration of how the courts apply this principle is *Thorpe* v *Frank* (2019) where the CA said that a key question was whether the claimant is doing that which an owner could do: if so, there is factual possession.

Note cases where there was no factual possession, e.g. *Techbild* v *Chamberlain Ltd* (1969) where playing on the land by children and tethering of ponies was not enough, and contrast that with cases where there was sufficient possession, e.g. *Williams* v *Usherwood* (1983), where the land was enclosed by a fence, three cars were parked on it and a driveway was paved. However, fencing is not always required: see *Thorpe* v *Frank* (2019) where repaving of land to enable car parking to continue on it established factual possession.

In *Rashid* v *Nasrullah* (2018) possession has initially been acquired by the fraud of the squatter's (X's) father in which X was complicit. The CA held that even if the doctrine of illegality applied, it would simply invalidate the registration. The fact would remain that X and his father had been in possession for the requisite period of time to claim by adverse possession.

Exam tip

Rather than learn many cases on what constitutes factual possession, it is better to be clear about what Slade J said (earlier) in *Powell* v *McFarlane* and apply this to the question.

Intention to possess

This is often referred to as the '*animus possidendi*'.

You need to deal with this separately from factual possession as it may be that, although there is factual possession, there is clearly no intention to possess.

Example 10.1

X is in occupation of a house which he has agreed to look after for a friend, while the friend is away on holiday. He may have factual possession, but he does not intend to actually possess it.

This example is from the speech of Lord Browne-Wilkinson in *Pye* v *Graham* in which he emphasised that intention to own is not required, only intention to possess. This means that the adverse possessor (AP) does not have to prove that he believed that the land was his (he knows that it is not his anyway) but that he intended to exclude the paper owner. In fact, as Lord Hutton observed in *Pye*, the facts of an intention to possess will be often deduced from the acts of control.

In *Alston and Sons Ltd* v *BOCM Pauls Ltd* (2008) it was held that it is sufficient where the intention is to possess indefinitely, coupled if possible, with an acceptance that the property would have to be given back if the owner demanded it.

Section 144 of the Legal Aid, Sentencing and Punishment of Offenders Act 2012 creates the offence of squatting in a residential building where the defendant 'knows or ought to know' of his or her trespassing. In *Best* v *Chief Land Registrar* (2015) the CA confirmed the decision of the High Court that a person who is committing an offence under section 144 is not debarred from claiming title by adverse possession under the LRA 2002.

Don't be tempted to . . .

Confuse possession where it is adverse with possession where the possessor intends to acquire an easement by prescription (see Chapter 8). In *Best* v *Chief Land Registrar* (2014) Ouseley J in the High Court pointed out the fundamental difference: prescription involves lawful 'possession as of right', based on the presumed intention of the landowner to grant title, while adverse possession involves 'possession as of wrong'. In addition, an easement is not a claim to exclusive use: an adverse possession claim is.

Earmarked land

This follows from the previous point. Can an AP intend to possess where he is aware that the paper owner had a future intended use? It follows that he can, as it is sufficient if he intends to exclude the paper owner. The present law is now clear and easily recognised in exams. It is illustrated by the following case.

Buckinghamshire County Council v *Moran* [1989] 2 All ER 225 (CA)

Facts
The defendant enclosed land belonging to the claimant and treated it as an extension of his garden. The claimant had intended to use the land to carry out a road diversion.

Legal principle
The fact that the paper owner had a future intended use for the land for a road diversion did not stop the defendant from adversely possessing it.

Analysis
This important decision overruled the 'implied licence' theory (see *Leigh* v *Jack* (1879)) that the claimant was assumed to have been given an implied licence to use the land provided his actions were not inconsistent with an intended use by the owner. The effect of this was that if the possessor's actions were inconsistent with the owner's intended use then there could be no adverse possession. This was overruled. Do note, however, that Slade LJ said that in some limited circumstances the paper owner's future intended for the land might be relevant.

Impress your examiner

The most recent case in this area is *Pye* v *Graham* (discussed earlier) where the HL held that it would only be very occasionally that the fact that there is an intended future use will prevent adverse possession. Note also *Beulane Properties* v *Palmer* (2006), where there was a (probably short-lived) attempt to reintroduce the concept of earmarking for future use in the context of the Human Rights Act.

Don't be tempted to . . .

Be careful that you check if land has been earmarked for future use, e.g. Jack occupied land belonging to Sarah who intended to use it at some future date as a horse-riding establishment. This earmarking of land is usually irrelevant today (see above) and so almost certainly (see *Pye* v *Graham*) will not affect the outcome of your answer, but it could have prevented acquisition of title by Jack until the *Moran* case. Make this clear!

Acknowledgement of the paper owner's title

This point often arises in exam questions and is easily recognised.

Example 10.2

X has occupied a house belonging to Y for the past nine years and has treated it as his own. Y then says to X that he owes rent for the use of the house. An exam situation may say that either:

- X agrees to pay rent to Y; or
- X actually pays rent to Y and becomes Y's tenant.

In the second situation, X is clearly no longer an adverse possessor, as he has become Y's tenant. It is impossible to be both at the same time; otherwise all tenants would claim ownership by adverse possession.

It is the first example which has caused difficulty.

Pye v Graham [2002] 3 All ER 865 (HL)

Facts

The defendant occupied fields owned by the claimant under a licence and when this expired the defendant asked for a further licence which the paper owner refused to grant. The defendant remained in occupation.

Legal principle

Lord Browne-Wilkinson held that 'there is no inconsistency between a squatter being willing to pay the paper owner if asked and his being in the meantime in possession'. The point is that an intention to own is not required. If it was, willingness to pay would be fatal to a claim because why should I pay someone else for what I claim to own?

Analysis

This illustrates a fundamental point which you need to be absolutely clear on: in adverse possession cases the squatter cannot intend to own the land because she knows that it belongs to the paper owner. It is possession, not ownership, that matters.

What if the paper owner *unilaterally* grants a licence to the squatter? In *BP Properties Ltd* v *Buckler* (1988) it was held that this terminated any adverse possession and this was accepted as correct in *Smith* v *Molyneaux* [2016].

Adverse possession of a lease

This presents a different problem in one way, although the basic requirements for adverse possession remain.

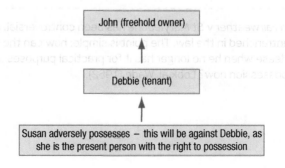

Unregistered

- If Susan adversely possesses, she has the right to possession, but this does not end Debbie's lease, so Debbie remains liable on the lease.

- Susan is not an assignee of the lease and so cannot be sued directly on the covenants in it.

- If Debbie breaches the covenants in the lease, John may claim to forfeit it. This will then give John the immediate right to possession and so he can then eject Susan.

- Time does not begin to run against John until the lease expires, but if Susan remains in possession she may, on the expiry of at least a further 12 years from the end of the lease, claim John's freehold.

- John can also bring forward the time when he can bring possession proceedings to evict Susan by taking a surrender of the lease from Debbie even though Susan has 12 years' adverse possession (*Fairweather* v *St Marylebone Property Co. Ltd* (1962)).

Registered

There will be a transfer of the lease as the squatter can be registered as owner of it, and so the squatter as the new tenant will be bound by the covenants in it. Meanwhile it appears that it will be possible *before* the squatter is registered as owner for the landlord to take a surrender of the lease under the principles in *Fairweather*. This will not be possible *after* registration as the (now) former tenant has nothing to surrender.

Note that a tenant, in her capacity of tenant, may adversely possess land belonging to a third party. If so, freehold title will pass not to the tenant, but to the landlord. See Lees (2015).

Impress your examiner

The decision in *Fairweather* v *St Marylebone* has been controversial, although is now firmly entrenched in the law. The point is simple: how can the tenant surrender the lease when he no longer has it for practical purposes as the squatter has possession now? Look at Wade (1962).

Applications to be registered as proprietor: unregistered land

When the period of 12 years is completed, the AP becomes entitled to be the owner. There is no actual process as such but the AP will need to prove to whomever he sells to that he is indeed the owner. He takes the land subject to all existing rights.

Applications to be registered as proprietor: the scheme of the LRA 2002 (Sch. 6, LRA 2002)

By contrast with the position where title is unregistered, the new scheme has a number of safeguards for the existing proprietor. In a problem question you will first need to establish that there is a right to be registered (factual possession plus intention to possess) as this is not affected by the LRA 2002. Only after you have dealt with this should you go through the procedures under this scheme.

Note these abbreviations:

AP: adverse possessor

RP: registered proprietor.

Summary of the scheme

Impress your examiner

The Law Commission, in its Report (2018) Updating Land Registration (LC 380), felt that no major changes were needed to this scheme but there were some points of detail on which fresh legislation was proposed. One was that where the reasonable belief of the squatter that the land belonged to him had ended, having existed for ten years, then there should be a time limit of six months for him to bring proceedings for registration.

Another was to deal with repeated applications for registration where the first one was rejected. Here the applicant might, on knowing that the RP was abroad and thus perhaps unable to reply in time, suddenly make a fresh application. Instead the Law Commission recommended that the applicant should have to remain in adverse possession for two more years before making another application.

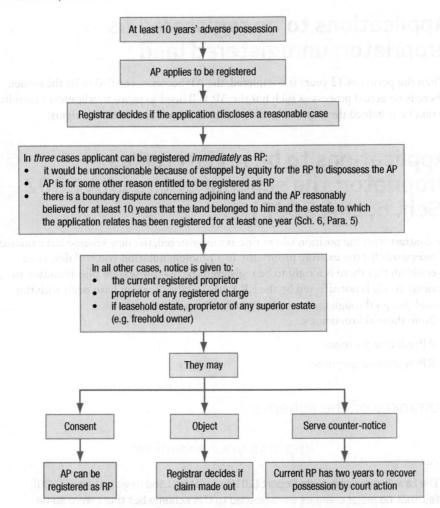

At least 10 years' adverse possession

AP applies to be registered

Registrar decides if the application discloses a reasonable case

In *three* cases applicant can be registered *immediately* as RP:
- it would be unconscionable because of estoppel by equity for the RP to dispossess the AP
- AP is for some other reason entitled to be registered as RP
- there is a boundary dispute concerning adjoining land and the AP reasonably believed for at least 10 years that the land belonged to him and the estate to which the application relates has been registered for at least one year (Sch. 6, Para. 5)

In all other cases, notice is given to:
- the current registered proprietor
- proprietor of any registered charge
- if leasehold estate, proprietor of any superior estate (e.g. freehold owner)

They may

Consent	Object	Serve counter-notice
AP can be registered as RP	Registrar decides if claim made out	Current RP has two years to recover possession by court action

---

Zarb v *Parry* [2011] EWCA 1306

Facts

There was a boundary dispute between two neighbouring houses. The adverse possessors, the Parrys, claimed that they, and their predecessors in title, had been in possession of a strip of land and that, under Schedule 6, Paragraph 5(4), they reasonably believed that it belonged to them.

Legal principle

Their belief was reasonable and so the claim succeeded. They knew that there had been a boundary dispute when they bought the property but thought that it had been resolved. Moreover, the Parrys had not received any communication from the paper owners, the Zarbs, and finally a report by a jointly commissioned surveyor concluded that the strip was in fact owned by the Parrys.

Analysis

Boundary disputes and the question of the reasonableness of the AP's belief are starting to generate case law. Note also *IAM Group Plc* v *Chowdrey* (2012) where it was held that it might be reasonable in these cases to make enquiries of your solicitors when you buy the land to see whether there has been a boundary dispute.

Note the following extra points:

- No application can be made when the current RP is unable, because of mental disability, to either make decisions on an application or to communicate those decisions (Sch. 6, Para. 8(2)). Exam questions sometimes raise this issue by telling you that the RP is ill or abroad. This does not by itself involve Schedule 6, Paragraph 8(2).

- The AP takes subject to all existing legal and equitable rights in the land except registered charges (Sch. 6, Paras 9(2) and (3)). This is why a registered chargee is entitled to be served with notice of an application so that it can object. The only exceptions are where the AP is registered as the RP in one of the three special cases discussed earlier. Here he or she will take subject to the charge.

- The AP can rely on periods of possession by another AP, e.g. X adversely possesses for five years and then dies but Y, her son, who had lived with her, continues the AP (Sch. 6, Para. 11, LRA 2002).

Adverse possession – change of squatter and paper owner

This point often appears in an exam problem question.

How to deal with this:

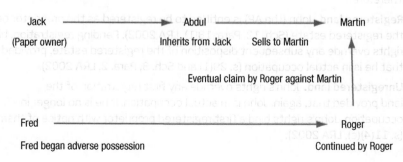

205

- It is assumed that between them Fred and Roger have 10 years' adverse possession.
- This must be continuous possession.
- If so, Roger can rely on Fred's previous periods of possession (Sch. 6, Para. 11, LRA 2002, and see diagram).
- Abdul is a donee.
- He is bound by any rights in the land and this includes rights in the course of being acquired by adverse possession – often known (although not strictly) as a mini-fee simple. As the disposition to him was not for valuable consideration, it is governed by section 28 of the LRA 2002. You should check that you know exactly why Abdul's rights are governed by section 28 (see Chapter 2).
- Martin is a purchaser. His rights are governed by section 29, LRA 2002. You should check that you know exactly why his rights are governed by section 29 (see Chapter 2).
- Any rights in the course of being acquired by adverse possession count as overriding interests under Schedule 3, Paragraph 2, LRA 2002, so the question is whether Martin is actually bound. Would Roger's occupation have been obvious on a reasonably careful inspection? Did Roger fail to disclose it when he could reasonably have been expected to? This is an absolutely vital point and is often completely missed by students. Do revise your knowledge of Schedule 3, paragraph 2 of the LRA in Chapter 2.

Watch for where the AP has completed the requisite period of possession before the commencement of the LRA 2002 on 13 October 2003.

Example 10.3

John began to adversely possess land belonging to Michael in 1990. By 13 October 2003, John will have completed the required period of adverse possession whether the title is registered (basic period of 12 years) or unregistered (12 years).

This point may still occur in exam questions, as a claim based on adverse possession may be made some years after the basic period for possession has been completed.

Therefore:

- **Registered land.** John (the AP) is entitled to be registered as the proprietor of the registered estate (Sch. 12, Para. 18(1), LRA 2002). Pending registration, his rights override any subsequent disposition of the registered estate, provided that he is in actual occupation (s. 29(1) and Sch. 3, Para. 2, LRA 2002).

- **Unregistered land.** John's rights override any first registration of the land provided that, again, John is in actual occupation. If he is no longer in occupation, John's rights bind a first registered proprietor with notice of them (s. 11(4)(c), LRA 2002).

Effect of the Human Rights Act (HRA)

The relevant part of the ECHR (enshrined in the HRA) is Article 1 of the First Protocol: you should know all of it but the vital part here is: 'No one shall be deprived of the peaceful enjoyment of his possessions except in the public interest and subject to the conditions provided for by law and the general principles of international law.'

In *J.A. Pye (Oxford) Ltd* v *UK* (2007) (see box earlier in this chapter for facts) the Grand Chamber of the ECtHR held that UK law does not infringe the ECHR and found that adverse possession was a justified control of use of land rather than a deprivation of possession and this was within the margin of appreciation. In *Ofulue* v *Bossert* (2008) the CA followed this reasoning and held that the principles of adverse possession law were compliant with human rights law.

Putting it all together

Sample question

Could you answer this question? What follows is a typical problem question that could arise on this topic. Additionally, a sample essay question and guidance on tackling it are included on the companion website.

Problem question

In 2006 Amy started to cultivate a field behind her house. She planted vegetables and later she erected a shed to store her gardening tools. Later on she also planted a hedge along the boundary to act as a windbreak. The registered owner of the field was Robert, who lived in France.

On a day visit to inspect his property Robert told Amy that he had no present use for the field but that he intended at some future time to seek planning permission to build on it. Meanwhile, he told Amy that he would be prepared to grant her a short lease. Amy told him to write to her solicitor about this but, although negotiations followed, no lease was ever granted.

Amy died in 2010, leaving all her property to her son Christopher, who had lived with her. Robert died in 2011, leaving all his property to his daughter Sally. Sally has had poor health and lives in a nursing home.

It is now 2018 and Christopher asks your advice on whether he can be registered as owner of the field and, if so, on the procedures that will apply.

Answer guidelines

Approaching the question

This question involves a number of issues all revolving around adverse possession. Make sure that you deal with all in full as they are not particularly difficult in themselves and so you could pick up a really good mark.

Important points to include

- Begin by checking dates and whether title is registered: it is, so initial period of 10 years and here it is now 2018 and Amy's possession began in 2006.
- Now check if Amy had factual possession and intention to possess for this time: look carefully at facts and compare with cases. May be doubtful whether she has, but note that it is now 12 years since Amy began the acts, which together may amount to possession. The planting of the hedge was later.
- Significance of negotiations for lease: note *Pye* v *Graham*.
- Deal with relevance of earmarking.
- Christopher takes over Amy's claim: Schedule 6, Paragraph 11, LRA 2002.
- Sally inherits the land: section 28, LRA 2002.
- Sally's health: Schedule 6, Paragraph 8(2), LRA 2002.
- Application for registration: procedures in Schedule 6, LRA 2002.

Impress your examiner

- -

Discuss the possible impact of the Human Rights Act (HRA) – see *Pye* v *Graham* and the discussion in this chapter and make sure that you actually relate the question to the HRA and do not just mention it!

Key case summary

Key case	How to use	Related topics
Pye J.A. (Oxford) Ltd v *Graham*	To show what can constitute factual possession.	Intention to possess.
Buckinghamshire County Council v *Moran*	To show that in general there is no principle that a claim to adverse possession can be defeated by showing that the paper owner had a future intended use for the land.	Earmarking.
Pye J.A. (Oxford) Ltd v *Graham*	To show that an intention to own the land is not required for a claim for adverse possession to succeed.	Intention to possess.
Zarb v *Parry*	To explain how Schedule 6, Paragraph 5(4) of the LRA works.	Adverse possession under the LRA 2002.

Key further reading

Key articles/reports	How to use	Related topics
Kerridge, R. and Brierley, A. (2007) Adverse possession, human rights and land registration: and they all lived happily ever after? 71 *Conv.* 552.	This is especially valuable in looking at the possible relevance of the Human Rights Act.	Adverse possession. Human Rights and Land Law.

▶

Key articles/reports	How to use	Related topics
Law Commission (1998) Paper 254, Land registration for the 21st century. Paras 10.5–10.78.	This is vital reading as it sets out the pervious law and the Law Commission's thinking behind the law which eventually resulted in the LRA 2002.	Adverse possession.
Law Commission Report (2018) Updating land registration. (LC) 380.	There are various recommendations for updating the procedure for acquiring title see Chapter 7 – pages 371–402.	Procedure for acquiring title by an AP.
Wade, H. (1962) Landlords, tenants and squatters. 78 *LQR* 541.	This article is strongly critical of the decision in *Fairweather* v *St Marylebone Property Co. Ltd* (1962)). Although it concerned unregistered land its principles have some application to registered land and so this decision and this article will continue to be important.	Adverse possession of leases.

go.pearson.com/uk/lawexpress

Go online to access more revision support including quizzes to test your knowledge, sample questions with answer guidelines, printable versions of the topic maps, and more!

Glossary of terms

The glossary is divided into two parts: key definitions and other useful terms. The key definitions can be found within the chapter in which they occur as well as in the glossary here. These definitions are the essential terms that you must know and understand in order to prepare for an exam. The additional list of terms provides further definitions of useful terms and phrases which will also help you answer examination and coursework questions effectively. These terms are highlighted in the text as they occur but the definition can only be found here.

Key definitions

Bare licences	Licences given without any consideration from the licensee, i.e. when you are invited to someone's house for a party.
Contractual licence	Where a licence is given for valuable consideration.
Corporeal hereditaments	The land and what is attached to the land.
Covenant	Promises in a deed.
Easement	Confers the right to use the land of another in some way or to prevent it from being used for certain purposes, e.g. rights of way and rights of water and light.
Equitable interests	This term means that the right was originally only recognised by the Court of Chancery, which dealt with equitable rights, and not by the Courts of Common Law.
Estate in land	Refers to the rights which a person has to control and use the land. An estate owner is often called the owner of the land.

Fee simple absolute in possession	Fee – can be inherited
	Simple – by anyone
	Absolute – will not end on a certain event, i.e. to X until he marries.
	In possession – not, e.g., to X at 21.
Fixtures and fittings	Fixtures are objects which are fixed to the land in such a way as to be part of it. Fittings are not.
Freehold	A legal estate in land which lasts for an unlimited time and in practice is perpetual.
Incorporeal hereditaments	Rights over land. Section 205(1)(ix) of the LPA 1925 provides that it means 'an easement, right, privilege, or benefit in, over, or derived from land'.
Injunction	A court order which either orders a lawful act to be done or restrains an unlawful act.
Interest in land	A right which a person has over another's land.
Joint tenancy	Where there are no shares, i.e. all the joint tenants own all the land jointly.
Land	'Land . . . and mines and minerals, whether or not held apart from the surface' – land is not just the actual surface but also land below and air space above. What is unsettled is how far it extends: the old phrase '*usque ad coelum et ad inferos*' (up to heaven and down to hell) is legally incorrect but the landowner does own at least some portion; otherwise it would be impossible to dig the ground and to erect a block of flats. Note *Bernstein* v *Skyviews and General Ltd* (1978) claim by a landowner for trespass in respect of flights over his house for aerial photography rejected: the court held that a landowner only owns such airspace necessary for the reasonable enjoyment of the land.
Landlord and tenant	The parties to a lease are the landlord and the tenant, but they are legally the lessor (landlord) and the lessee (tenant).
Lease	An estate in land which, therefore, gives a proprietory interest in the land.
Leasehold	A legal estate which lasts for a definite time.
Legal interests	These are defined in section 1(2) of the LPA 1925. Only these can be legal. All interests not in this list must be equitable. Legal interests bind all the world, i.e. everyone who buys the land.

Licence	Permission from an owner of land (licensor) to the licensee to use the land for a specific purpose.
Licence coupled with a grant	Where the licence is linked to an interest in the land, e.g. a licence to go on to land to collect wood. The right to collect wood is a profit.
Lost modern grant	The court assumes two things that have not, in fact, occurred: • there was a grant of an easement; • it has been lost.
Mere equity	Arises where there is a right in equity to apply for a remedy, such as specific performance of a contract for the sale of land or to set aside a contract on the ground that it is an unconscionable bargain or for misrepresentation or undue influence.
Misrepresentation	An untrue statement of fact which induces a person to enter into a transaction.
Mortgage	A charge on land to secure a debt.
Mortgagee	The lender in a mortgage is a mortgagee.
Mortgagor	The borrower in a mortgage is a mortgagor.
Negative covenant	One which restricts the use to which land can be put.
Overreaching	The process by which equitable rights which exist under a trust of land are removed from the land and transferred to the money (called capital money) which has been paid to purchase the land. The effect is to give the purchaser automatic priority over equitable interests under a trust.
Overriding interest	An unregistered disposition which overrides registered dispositions.
Parties to a lease	• **Lessor:** grantor of the lease. • **Lessee:** grantee of the lease. • **Headlease:** lease granted by the lessor to the lessee as distinct from a sub-lease. • **Freehold reversion:** the rights retained by the lessor on the grant of a lease. • **Assignment:** disposition of the lessee's interest to the assignee who then takes over the assignor's interest in the land. • **Underlease/sub-lease:** creation of a subsidiary estate out of the lessee's estate.

Personal rights	Those which are not capable of binding third parties, i.e. licences.
Prescription	Acquisition of easements and profits by long use.
Profits	Gives the right to take something from the land of another, e.g. peat, fish, wood or grazing rights.
Proprietary rights	Those which are capable of binding third parties, i.e. legal estates and legal and equitable interests in land.
Protected registered interests	Interests in land which are neither registrable dispositions nor overriding interests and include: covenants on freehold land; equitable easements and profits; estate contracts.
Registrable disposition	One that must be completed by registration.
Rentcharge	Gives the owner the right to a periodical sum of money secured on land independently of any lease or mortgage.
Restrictive covenant	Where a person covenants in a deed not to use his land in a certain way or to do something on his land, e.g. to keep fences in repair or not to build on the land.
Severance in equity	'Such acts or things as would, in the case of personal estate, sever the tenancy in equity' (*Williams* v *Hensman* (1861)).
Specific performance	A court order which commands the performance of a contract.
Tenancy at sufferance	Where the tenant, after the expiry of the lease, continues in possession without the consent of the landlord (remember that a tenant at will does have consent). A tenant at sufferance has no real tenancy and cannot even sue another for trespass.
Tenancy at will	Where the tenant, with the owner's consent, occupies land at the will of the owner who, therefore, may terminate it at any time.
	The tenant has no security of tenure and is really in no better position than a licensee.
Tenancy in common	Where the beneficial owners have shares in the land.
Term of years absolute	(In relation to a lease) any period having a fixed and certain duration. 'Absolute' appears to have no meaning beyond the fact that a term of years may be absolute even if it contains a clause enabling either party to determine it by notice.
Trust	Arises when property is held by one person (the trustee) on trust for another (the beneficiary).

Other useful terms

Assignment	Transfer of property such as, in land law, a lease.
Beneficiaries	Those who are entitled in equity to property which is held on trust and who therefore have the equitable (beneficial) interest in that property.
Commonhold	A method of holding freehold land used to enable the owners of flats to form a company which will hold the common parts (e.g. the stairs) as commonhold.
Deed	An instrument which makes it clear on its face that it is intended to be a deed and which satisfies the requirements for execution as a deed.
Equity	The body of rules developed and administered by the Court of Chancery.
Notice	Actual constructive or imputed notice which decides if a person is bound by an unregistered equitable interest.
Obiter	An observation made in a judgment which is not part of the actual decision in the case and so is not a precedent (in full, *obiter dicta*) but is often used as a guide to what the law might be.
Paper owner	The holder of the legal title to land which is being adversely possessed.
Periodic tenancy	A tenancy for a certain period (weekly, monthly quarterly, etc.) which is automatically renewed at the end of each period unless either party gives notice.
Registered proprietor	The person who is registered as the proprietor of land to which the title has been registered.
Remaindermen	Entitled to an estate in future on the termination of the estate of the previous owner, usually the holder of a life interest.
Severance	Where something is divided up, e.g. where a joint tenancy is divided into separate shares so that it becomes a tenancy in common.
Trustees	Those who hold property on trust for others who are the beneficiaries.

Index

Note: **Emboldened** entries refer to those appearing in the glossary

Index